T0093088

SECURITY IN IoT

SECURITY IN IoT

The Changing Perspective

Edited by
Rituparna Chaki &
Debdutta Barman Roy

CRC Press
Taylor & Francis Group
Boca Raton London New York

CRC Press is an imprint of the
Taylor & Francis Group, an **informa** business

First edition published 2022
by CRC Press
6000 Broken Sound Parkway NW, Suite 300, Boca Raton, FL 33487-2742
and by CRC Press

4 Park Square, Milton Park, Abingdon, Oxon, OX14 4RN

Library of Congress Cataloging-in-Publication Data

Names: Chaki, Rituparna, editor. | Roy, Debdutta Barman, editor. Title: Security in IoT / [edited by] Rituparna Chaki & Debdutta Barman Roy. Description: First edition. | Boca Raton : CRC Press, 2022. | Includes bibliographical references and index. | Summary: "The diverse applications of IoT are achieved by a set of complex inter-related networks of things and communications. IoT applications are also concerned about an array of devices such as sensors, mobile devices, personal computers, the smart systems such as Alexa, Eco, etc, besides the whole range of communication network binding them together in a seamless manner. This book explores the variegated perspectives of security in the complex context of Internet of Things. It also aims to present the changing face of security, from the ubiquitous networks comprising of WSN as the lowest layer, to the enabler apps working as bridge between the users and the complex IoT system. It takes a closer look at the different types of security schemes required to fit in the heterogeneous nature of IoT network, whilst the readers are also introduced to basic attacks targeting an IoT network, as well as specific types of security schemes worked out by researchers across different countries. As Programmable Logic Controllers (PLC) play a fundamental role in Industrial Control Systems, since they provide various functionalities of physical tools by collecting data from input devices and sending commands to output devices, this book includes a discussion on the security considerations of extending a PLC-based system with IoT capabilities. Other advanced topics include: The machine ethics aspects in the IoT system; the Intrusion detection of WSN; and the methods of securing the user from privacy breaches due to the overprivileged IoT apps. This book will be beneficial to any readers interested in security of IoT systems and how to develop a layer-wise security scheme for such a system"-- Provided by publisher. Identifiers: LCCN 2021043044 (print) | LCCN 2021043045 (ebook) | ISBN 9780367711412 (hbk) | ISBN 9780367711429 (pbk) | ISBN 9781003149507 (ebk) Subjects: LCSH: Internet of things--Security measures. Classification: LCC TK5105.8857 .S448 2022 (print) | LCC TK5105.8857 (ebook) | DDC 004.67/8--dc23/eng/20211103 LC record available at https://lccn.loc.gov/2021043044 LC ebook record available at https://lccn.loc.gov/2021043045

ISBN: 9780367711412 (hbk)
ISBN: 9780367711429 (pbk)
ISBN: 9781003149507 (ebk)

DOI: 10.1201/9781003149507

Typeset in Adobe Caslon Pro
by KnowledgeWorks Global Ltd.

To my dear baba for his belief in me

Contents

List of Figures and Tables

Background

Nowadays, we are moving toward a world composed of many sensors, and all these sensors can communicate among themselves using the Internet. Internet of Things (IoT) is an entirely new research domain that has emerged from this. IoT is a system of interrelated computing devices, and with its rapid development and distribution came into focus an interest by Internet users, especially users of smart devices.

This is supported by the fact that the IoT is not only limited to mechanical and digital machines, but also covers other objects, animals, and even people who are provided with unique identifiers that have an ability to transfer data over a network. The major challenges that are faced in the development of IoT may be listed as:

1. Deployment of nodes: In contrast to the traditional networks where the topology of the network was known exactly before establishment of the network, it is very difficult in WSN, which is an important component of IoT, to keep the topology fixed as the nodes are deployed randomly on the field.

2. Heterogeneous devices: Devices differ according to the types of network standards they use and the types of applications they support. Also, these devices can be different in terms of their resources. Some devices suffer from resource constraints and some do not.

3. Diverse networking standards: IoT is an umbrella that brings various technologies, such as traditional network, WSN, Zigbee, WiFi, etc., together. The working principles of these technologies are diverse. They use different protocol stacks.

4. Intermittent connectivity: Due to limited battery life, there is always a danger of change in the network topology. Intermittent connectivity can also be experienced due to highly mobile devices, which get disconnected from the network when they move.

5. Multi-hop communication: Most of the devices used in IoT are low-powered devices. These devices are short-range transmitting devices, and thus they use a relay mechanism while transmitting the data from source to destination.

6. Fault tolerance: Due to environmental factors, deployment mechanisms, or energy constraints, there is always a danger of affecting the overall network performance. So, there must be some mechanism in the routing protocols to handle such unexpected events.

7. Security: Because of some dishonest participants, routing security issues arise. Hop-to-hop authentication is not enough. Cryptography can mitigate the effects to some extent but not completely.

8. Context awareness: An IoT application includes voice assistants (Alexa, Google home, etc.), that perform different actions based on a user's spoken commands. Often similar sounding commands need to be interpreted differently based on their context. In such context-aware environments, the system must use context information for making necessary changes in the routing process. The different aspects of context-aware computing include mainly five sub-technologies: (1) getting context, (2) context-modeling, (3) context-reasoning, (4) context-conflict solving, and (5) context-storage and management.

Guidance from the Author

This book discusses the evolution of security schemes from the days of wireless sensor network to present all-pervasive, all-inclusive concepts of Internet of Things, or IoT as it is popularly called.

The book is planned for someone interested in working in the domain of IoT security and, yet quite confused by the array of possible security breaches affecting different parts of IoT. Here, an attempt is made to help the reader with a look into the most basic form of security needed by an IoT environment as well as the other layers. We aim to empower the reader with sufficient insight and experience to design security techniques aimed toward securing the overall IoT environment, including its users. This book would be good as part of a course for a first-year master's student. As a researcher, you may prefer to go beyond that and prepare yourself to get into depth of understanding of the challenges.

There is a lot to learn, and you will be threading through the different security schemes existing at different layers of IoT. The book has a medium speed flow, with each chapter introducing a different aspect of IoT security and explains them with cases built on real-life applications. You will slowly learn the transition from the lowest layer of IoT security concerning the sensor network security to the highest layer concerning enabler app security. We would like to help you in identifying and understanding the probable security breaches at different layers of IoT networks and then learn to mitigate them one by one in order to generate a complete security solution.

Why would you be interested in this book? As a student of computing, you know that our lives rely on IoT to a large extent for making life easier. It is a well-known fact that in order to understand the 'magic' of Alexa, Siri, Cortana, etc., to name just a few of such 'smart' companions, you must understand the possible threats to us posed by their listen-always mode of operation. There are many other activities performed by the sensors and other enablers constituting an IoT system, which has the possibility of breaching user security. When we discuss IoT, we are concerned about the entire array of devices such as sensors, mobile devices, personal computers, and smart systems such as Alexa, Eco, etc. Besides a whole range of communication networks, it binds them together in a seamless manner.

While this is not the oldest book about IoT security, the book encompasses different types of security schemes worked out by researchers across different countries. I just aim for it to be the most useful book that gives you an idea of the layer-wise security requirements in an IoT network.

Organization

The first chapter, *Security Aspect in IoT,* is a short overview of application areas of IoT and security vulnerabilities of IoT. The chapter also discusses some of the existing techniques created to avoid these vulnerabilities in order to familiarize the reader with the basics.

The second chapter is *Robustness Analysis of PLC Programs with Respect to Sensor Interaction in IoT.* Industrial IoT applications depend heavily upon programmable logic controllers (PLC), which play a fundamental role in Industrial Control Systems. The PLCs provide various functionalities of physical tools by collecting data from input devices and sending commands to output devices. Thus, the robustness of PLC programs needs to be guaranteed to provide necessary basic security to the industrial IoT applications. In this chapter, the authors have discussed the issue of verification of the robustness of PLC programs. This includes (i) identifying *external vulnerabilities* based on dynamic user interactions, (ii) defining the semantics of Structured Control Language (SCL) and the semantics of Timed Automata (TA), (iii) a set of transformation rules provided to transform a program written in SCL to a TA, and (iv) showing their correctness with respect to the corresponding semantics. This is followed by the application of Model Checking tools to verify robustness properties of the PLC source code.

The third chapter, *Security of IoT,* discusses the ethical aspects toward design and implementation of IoT security frameworks. The chapter addresses ethical performance of intelligent agents interconnected in the IoT network. It discusses the concept of Machine Ethics (ME), which involves adding moral behaviors to machines comprising an IoT network that use artificial intelligence (AI). The issues of ME from the IoT perspective are revised, and recent undertakings of multidisciplinary bodies to counter ethical threats in AI and IoT are recalled.

The fourth chapter, *An Intrusion Detection System for WSN Layer of IoT,* discusses the base layer security approach in an IoT network. As sensors comprise the lowest layer of perception in IoT environments, the security at this layer is most important to guarantee the correctness of information being transmitted to the higher layers of IoT networks. Intrusion detection systems (IDS) form an integral part of a generic IoT security scheme. This chapter discusses the Distributed Denial-of-Service (DDOS) attack and talks about the disruption caused by it to the lowest layer of IoT networks, the wireless sensor network (WSN). The IDS is implemented using the concept of Mobile Agents here. These mobile agents have been used to help prolong the lifetime of the network besides speedy detection of intrusion within the network.

The fifth and final chapter is *An NLP-Based Scheme for User Data Security from Overprivileged IoT Apps.* The issue of application-level security has been the topic of discussion in the final chapter. This discusses the topic of IoT security from a user perspective. The enabler applications of IoT require several specific permissions at the time of installation for seamless performance. Many of the applications pose serious security threats to a user's private data due to the nature of permissions sought at install time. The chapter addresses the concern of user security breach due to overprivileged IoT enabler apps. In this context, a framework based on natural language processing (NLP) tools is described, which is used for reviewing the application descriptions to warn the users before installing an app.

Acknowledgments

I would especially like to thank my co-researcher Prof. Agostino Cortesi, Ca Foscari University, Venice, for encouraging me to tackle the difficult task of continuing to write the book through the days of the pandemic. We have learnt to change our priorities in these two years as life has changed unexpectedly. The gentle nudges from Tino made me go back to the book again and again.

Nabendu, my husband and colleague, has been a constant support and pillar of strength all through the writing of the book. I take this opportunity to thank him for his valuable inputs.

I acknowledge with thanks my children, Tintin and Khushi, for their understanding and loving support while I was busy working on the manuscript.

Rituparna Chaki

1

SECURITY OF IoT

EŞREF ADALI

Istanbul Technical University Istanbul, Turkey

Contents

DOI: 10.1201/9781003149507-1

1

1.1 Introduction

In the 1970s, the favorite subject of the control field was Distributed Computer Control (DCC). DCC reduced costs of cabling and offered more successful control. Microprocessors provided this opportunity to DCC. DCC has been widely used in iron and steel factories, rolling mills, pipe lines, traffic control system, Supervisory Control and Data Acquisition (SCADA) and in vehicle control systems. In these applications, dedicated star and ring-shaped networks are used for communication between sensors, actuators and controllers. Some communication protocols have also been developed in this area [1, 2]. In applications where the distances are relatively short, cable is preferred, and wireless connection is used for long distances.

Nowadays, the concept of DCC has been greatly expanded and has become a form where everything in the world can be monitored and controlled. In the new application, the connections between the sensors, controller and actuators are provided over the Internet. That's why it's called the Internet of Things (IoT). IoT makes possible

Industry 4.0, smart/green cities, smart building/homes, autonomy vehicles, utility meters, etc. The Internet has provided a very cheap communication medium between those who control and who are controlled.

1.1.1 IoT Definition

There are several definitions of IoT. One of them is as follows [3]:

> *An open and comprehensive network of intelligent objects that has the capacity to auto organize, share information, data and resources, reacting and acting in face of situations and changes in the environment.*

We can consider IoT as a worldwide network which allows communication between things–things, things–human and human–human. In short, it is a communication network that connects everything in the world. Things can perceive the physical features of their environment with their sensors and share the obtained data with other things on the network. In addition, they can control their environment with actuators.

According to the research results of Cisco, the increasing trend of IoT devices over the years is shown in Figure 1.1 [4].

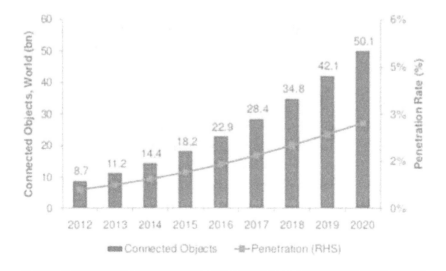

Figure 1.1   Expected penetration of connected objects by the year 2020, Cisco.

1.2 Application of IoT

IoT has several applications in different areas. These applications can be classified as follows [5–8]:

- Industry/Production
- Transportation
- Healthcare
- Governance
- City and communities
- Home and office
- Consumer or the users
- Supply chain
- Agriculture

1.2.1 Industrial/Production

Nowadays, dark factories or, more generally, Industry 4.0 is a topic of discussion. Industry 4.0 is a very good example of IoT. In Industry 4.0, the communication between production devices and systems controlling them is provided over the Internet. Those who control the system will work outside the factory in an office environment.

1.2.2 Transportation

Transportation is one of the promising areas where IoT can be used. The conditions under which transportation vehicles operate, their positions and speeds can be monitored from a center, which will provide significant benefits. The information obtained from the vehicles can be used in two ways: Providing transportation information to the citizens and managing the vehicles in the best way to the people who govern the city.

Nowadays, we are witnessing the development of autonomous vehicles. Autonomous vehicles must communicate with each other and the urban traffic system. IoT-based systems will be suitable for this communication.

1.2.3 Healthcare

IoT offers new possibilities for continuous monitoring of people with chronic diseases. Wearable sensors enable continuous monitoring of health information of such patients. These collected data can be transferred to a specialist doctor for quick and necessary medical intervention.

1.2.4 Governance

The consolidation of a large amount of varied data collected by IoT can be an important resource for decision-makers. The data in question can be in the form of weather, financial records and security data.

1.2.5 City and Communities

Nowadays, more and more urban planners are trying to build smart cities, smart buildings, smart homes and smart offices. The smart city concept is used in two areas: Smart traffic and green city. The basic idea behind smart cities is to save time and money by controlling the traffic flow. Intelligent traffic system provides convenience, time and economic gain for citizens and their country. Green city practice mainly deals with the management of air pollution. It is known that air pollution is related to urban vehicle trailer.

When the heating/cooling and lighting systems in a building are IoT-based, it becomes easy to manage and maintain them. We can also add security and fire systems to these systems. The purpose of establishing a smart building is to prevent unnecessary energy use, thus providing economy.

Smart parking is another example of an IoT system. The smart parking system offers drivers suitable parking spaces, avoiding wastage of time and unnecessary fuel consumption by searching for parking spaces in the city.

IoT systems are used for efficient use of electricity distribution networks, ensuring security and real-time monitoring. We are witnessing IoT solution examples for water distribution systems. These applications are called smart grid.

1.2.6 Home and Office

Nowadays, it is aimed to connect white goods and entertainment systems with each other and to manage them from a single point. To achieve this goal, all devices (home appliances, TV, speaker, game systems, etc.) must be IoT-based. Heating/cooling and security systems in the house can also be considered within this scope.

If the devices used in office and homes are IoT-based devices, the maintenance services of these devices will be faster and better. As a result, customers will be satisfied and the producers will be less expensive to service. The following example explains the subject very well: One day your door is knocked and you shouldn't be surprised when you see a service man. Because the service man will tell you that your air conditioner is due for maintenance and that is why he has arrived.

1.2.7 Supply Chain

The use of smart sensors such as Radio Frequency Identification (RFID) and Near Field Communication (NFC) and their ability to communicate with the IoT systems have made significant contributions to supply chains. With this application method, all products in the chain can be traced from the source to the customer.

1.2.8 Agriculture

IoT solutions make significant contributions to the field of agriculture. The temperature, humidity and chemicals in the soil in a field or greenhouse can be measured. The results of these measurements can be evaluated, and necessary irrigation, heating and fertilization can be done.

1.3 Security Issues of IoT

The communication medium used in DCC applications was private, so it was difficult to access this network from outside. In addition, the equipment used was application-specific and was developed for industrial use, so its reliability was high. Similarly, the software used was developed sufficiently reliably. The communication techniques and protocols used in DCC were developed specifically for the application and were extremely robust in terms of security.

Security issues are listed below, and detailed information is given in the upcoming sections:

- Communication medium and protocol
- Hardware and software
- Weakness against cyberattacks
- Monitoring devices
- Data protection
- Autonomous systems

1.3.1 Communication Medium and Protocol

IoT uses the Internet as a communication medium; therefore, it is open and vulnerable to attacks. In order to make the communication over the Internet more reliable, some special protocols and techniques are added to find a better solution.

There are two important things about the data transfer over the Internet: The data is transferred in a short time and it is not corrupted during communication. The access of the data sent over the Internet to the other party depends on the bandwidth of the Internet used and the usage density of the network. Especially in time-critical applications, communication speed, or in other words, delay on the Internet, can be an important problem.

Data sent over the Internet is likely to be corrupted. A suitable method can be used to solve this problem.

1.3.2 Hardware and Software

The hardware and software used in IoT can be divided into two clusters: Central units and terminal units; these are mostly called IoT devices. IoT devices are numerous and take on the task of data collection and control of actuators. Most of the hardware developed for IoT devices do not meet the industry requirement. In addition, it cannot be said that the software developed for this hardware is sufficient for security. Some hardware and software can be considered safe as of the moment they are produced, but security vulnerabilities emerge over time and therefore they need to be updated.

Cyber attackers are constantly investigating how to capture IoT devices. Attackers use measures and countermeasure approaches.

Therefore, they can find out new techniques or methods for security threats. For this reason, the software developed should be able to protect the IoT device against such attacks, or the software should be updated frequently.

If the embedded software on the IoT device is not secure enough, malicious software can settle on the IoT device. Malware may alter the data collected from the field or cause actuators to malfunction. Ransomware gets control of the IoT devices and cuts off communication with the center and the other devices.

1.3.3 Weakness against Cyberattacks

The first reason for the vulnerability of IoT devices to cyberattacks is the use of factory settings. Most IoT devices are sold with weak and default (such as user name: Admin and passwords: 123456) identities for ease of use. This problem is called weak and default credentials. Since the majority of users do not reset username and password, the devices are used with factory settings, which makes it easier for the cyberattackers to capture devices.

1.3.4 Monitoring Devices

Some of the IoT devices connected to the system may be corrupted, some may be malfunctioning by malicious software or some may be captured by the ransomware program. It is necessary to constantly monitor whether all IoT devices connected to the system are intact and working properly. An advanced monitoring system needs to be set up to detect that all IoT devices connected to the network are working properly.

1.3.5 Data Protection

The Internet is a public communication medium, so there is always the possibility that data sent over the Internet could be stolen and altered. If the data gets leaked, the person who gets the data can use or sell it to other people or group parties who violate the rights for data privacy and security. Appropriate security algorithms must be used to ensure data security.

1.3.6 Autonomous Systems

The main idea is to manage IoT systems from a center.. This logic assumes that the Internet is always up and the data transfer is fast enough. However, there may be situations where the Internet may be cut off or blocked. In such cases, the system should be kept in working condition. For example, suppose the system that manages the city traffic is based on IoT. When the Internet connection between the center and the IoT devices at the intersections is disconnected, the IoT device at the junction should detect interruption, and in this case, it should execute the predefined program for this intersection.

A similar situation applies to recently developed smart vehicles. They act with data from other vehicles and the city traffic system. Since communication is provided over the Internet, smart cars should be able to manage themselves in case the Internet is cut or blocked.

1.4 Architecture of IoT

It can be seen that the architecture of the IoT is inspired by the Open Systems Interconnection (OSI) architecture. Some show it as three [3, 9] and five layers [10], and some as six layers [4]. The extended form of the Transmission Control Protocol/Internet Protocol (TCP/IP) is used to address things. This is because the number of IoT devices in the world is more than 20 billion and this number is increasing rapidly. The six-level architecture of IoT is shown in Figure 1.2 [3, 4, 10, 7].

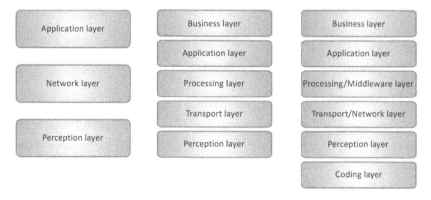

Figure 1.2   Architecture of IoT.

1.4.1 Coding Layer

The coding layer is the layer required to identify the IoT device. The unique identity of each IoT device is written on this layer.

1.4.2 Perception Layer

The perception layer is similar to the physical layer of an OSI model, which consists of different types of sensors and actuators. The sensors may be physical sensors such as temperature, speed and pressure sensors, or they may be digital sensors such as RFID and QR code sensors. This layer knows the properties of different sensors and evaluates the information these sensors collect from the environment. The information collected by the sensors can be various physical variables such as ambient temperature, ambient humidity, air pollution, light intensity, wind speed. This collected information is transferred to the network layer.

1.4.3 Network Layer

The task of the network layer is to ensure that the data from the perception layer is securely transferred to the communication environment. Data from the perception layer may be sensitive data, and this data must be delivered to the central system where it will be processed without being corrupted or stolen. IoT systems use different communication environments, for example, GSM Network (3G, 4G, 5G) Universal Mobile Telecommunications System (UMTS) Wi-Fi, Bluetooth, Worldwide Interoperability for Microwave Access (WiMAX), RFID, Infrared, Satellite, etc.

1.4.4 Middleware Layer

The middleware layer processes the data from the sensors. It keeps the data in its database. It hosts cloud computing and ubiquitous technologies. This layer has the capability to retrieve data and process and compute information and then make decision on the computational results.

1.4.5 Application Layer

The management of applications processed in the middleware layer is the task of the application layer. IoT applications can be in smart health, smart car, smart home, smart transportation, etc.

1.4.6 Business Layer

The functions of business layer cover all the IoT applications and service management. This layer can create report, graphs, flowchart, business models, etc. by using data received from the lower layer. Good analysis results will help the functional managers or executives to make more accurate decisions about the business strategies.

1.5 IoT Security Measures

In this section, security measures of IoT such as confidentiality, integrity, authentication, authorization, availability, non-repudiation will be discussed [11, 9].

1.5.1 Confidentiality

The data collected and stored by IoT devices can be sensitive data. The acquisition of this data by unauthorized persons or devices may cause security vulnerabilities. For example, medical, personal, industry and military data are highly sensitive and must be secured against unauthorized access. Similarly, control data sent to IoT devices can also be sensitive data. The data must be secured both ways. Data encryption can be considered as a solution for this.

1.5.2 Integrity

Communication between IoT devices can be wired or wireless. The integrity of the transmitted and stored data is important. The immutability of the data stored in an IoT device or transmitted between IoT devices is very important. Attacks on IoT systems may be aimed at changing the data stored in the IoT device and transmitted between the IoT devices. Methods such as horizontal and vertical parity bits,

Hamming distance, checksum and Cyclic Redundancy Check (CRC) can be used to ensure the integrity of the transmitted or stored data, or different methods can be used to ensure integrity. Inconsistencies that may occur in the data can cause huge effect in medical, military and commercial transactions.

1.5.3 Authentication

Each IoT device has a unique identity. An IoT device can be accessed with this TCP/IP-based credential. Changing the address of an IoT device by attackers causes serious problems. These types of attacks can be done by physical or cyber methods. Those who manufacture IoT devices give simple identities to the devices they produce at the factory. When these simple identities are not changed during implementation, they become an easy prey for attackers.

1.5.4 Authorization

Data collected from the environment by IoT devices should only be used by people or devices that have the right and authority to use this data. Similarly, information sent to an IoT device that will control the actuators should only be available to that IoT device. In other words, the information collected by the IoT device should not go to an unrelated IoT device. Similarly, data concerning an actuator should only go to the IoT device it is connected to.

1.5.5 Availability

An IoT device must be running at all times. The inoperative situation of an IoT device should be reported to other IoT devices. In this case, scenarios on how to continue the work should be prepared in advance. Attackers try to make IoT devices inaccessible or inoperable.

1.5.6 Non-repudiation

Denial of data transmitted between IoT devices is not a major problem in cross-device work, but it appears as a problem in communication between IoT devices and human. For example, such problems are experienced in electronic payment systems.

1.6 Threats and Attacks in IoT

IOT devices encounter active and passive attacks. Attacks can disrupt an IoT device, prevent it from operating or cause it to malfunction. Some attacks do not prevent the IoT system from working; they only steal information from the system. We can categorize security threats of IoT as cyber and physical.

1.6.1 Cyber Threats

Cyber threats can be classified as passive or active.

1.6.1.1 Passive Threats Passive attacks are usually carried out by eavesdropping through communication network. By eavesdropping through communication network environment of the IoT system, sensitive data are tried to be obtained. These data are then sold to others for benefit. For example, there are some reports that credit card information (each $1.50) and health information (each $50) are sold in this way [12].

1.6.1.2 Active Threats Active attacks take different forms. For example,

- Changing the configuration of the IoT device: Changing the ID and password of IoT device. Data may go to wrong devices.
- Controlling the communication: Changing the network configuration.
- Keeping the IoT device busy (Denial-of-Service [DoS]): Sending so many requests to IoT devices so keep the busy.
- Making the IoT device in malfunctioning: Inserting malicious software into the IoT system. This software will run a code injection attack.
- Changing data: Deleting, changing, manipulating or editing of data that are stored in IoT device or transmitted over network.
- Preventing the IoT device from working: In order to do this, attacker use ransomware. This program compresses all the programs and data with a certain password. A ransom is required to restore programs.

Razzaq et al. give a summary for attack type and their threat levels, which is shown in Table 1.1 [13]. Some improvements and simplifications have been made in the table by us.

1.6.2 Physical Threats

Attackers who are not capable of carrying out cyberattacks often make physical attacks. They acquire and break IoT devices and make them inaccessible.

1.6.3 Security Challenges in the Main Layers of IoT

In this section, some of the threats in each architectural layer that needs special attention are discussed. IoT security issues related the layer of IoT is described in this section.

1.6.3.1 Perception Layer   The task of the perception layer is perceiving and gathering information from environment by sensors and transferring it to the upper layer. Temperature sensors, pressure sensors, RFIDs and barcodes are some examples of sensors. The wireless nature of the signals makes this layer susceptible to attackers. The nodes and sensors mostly operate in an external environment and this cause culminates in physical attacks. The main problems are leakage of confidential information, tampering, terminal virus, copying and other issues [10]. Security issues with this layer are described below.

1.6.3.1.1 Unauthorized Access   The IDs and passwords of IoT devices are simple or the IDs and passwords set at the factory are used. Therefore, these devices are easy to access by unauthorized persons.

1.6.3.1.2 Node Capture   An attacker can capture nodes or devices in the IoT system. Then it can go to ID replication by generating new IDs for IoT devices. This attack can have serious effects.

1.6.3.1.3 Tag Cloning   For example, RFID tags attached to IoT devices are visible. The tags can be cloned and connected to the IoT device as original. The cloned tag can generate different information, which can lead to negative consequences.

Table 1.1 Different Types of Attacks and Their Threat Levels, Types and Suggested Solutions

TYPE	THREAT LEVEL	BEHAVIOR	SUGGESTED SOLUTION
Passive	Low	Usually breach data confidentiality. Examples are passive eavesdropping and traffic analysis. Hostile silently listens the communication for his own benefits without altering the data.	Ensure confidentiality of data and do not allow an attacker to fetch information using encryption techniques.
Man in the middle	Low to medium	The attacker secretly relays and possibly alters the communications between two parties who believe that they are directly communicating with each other.	Apply data confidentiality and proper integration on data to ensure integrity. Encryption can also be applied so that no one can steal the information or modify.
Eavesdropping	Low to medium	The information content may be stolen by an eavesdropper. For example, in medical environment, privacy of a patient may be leaked.	Apply encryption on all the devices that perform communication.
Gathering	Medium to high	Data is gathered from different wireless or wired medium. Examples are skimming, tampering and eavesdropping.	Encryption can be applied to prevent this kind of attack. Identity-based method and message authentication code can also be applied in order to prevent the network from such malicious attacks.
Active	High	Effects confidentiality and integrity of data. Hostile can alter the integrity of messages, block messages or may reroute the messages.	To maintain data confidentiality, encryption can be applied. An authentication mechanism may be applied to allow data access to only authorized person.
Imitation	High	It impersonates for an unauthorized access. Spoofing and cloning are the examples of this attack. In spoofing attack, a malicious node impersonates any other device and launches attacks to steal data or to spread malware. Cloning can rewrite or duplicate data.	To avoid from spoofing and cloning attacks, apply identity-based authentication protocols. Physically unclonable function is a countermeasure for cloning attack.

(Continued)

Table 1.1 (Continued) Different Types of Attacks and Their Threat Levels, Types and Suggested Solutions

TYPE	THREAT LEVEL	BEHAVIOR	SUGGESTED SOLUTION
Privacy	High	Sensitive information of an individual or group may be disclosed. Such attacks may be correlated to gathering attack or may cause an imitation attack that can further lead to exposure of privacy.	Apply anonymous data transmission. Transmit sample data instead of actual data. Can also apply techniques like ring signature and blind signature.
Interruption	High	Affects availability of data. This makes the network unavailable.	Applying authorization. Only authorized users are allowed to access specific information to perform certain operation.
Routing diversion	High	Only the route is diverted showing the huge traffic and the response time increased.	Ensure connectivity-based approach, so no route will be diverted.
Blocking	Extremely high	It is type of DoS, jamming, or malware attacks. It sends huge streams of data which may lead to jamming of network, similarly different types of viruses like Trojan horses, worms and other programs can disturb the network.	Turn on the firewall, apply packet filtering, anti-jamming, active jamming and updated antivirus programs in order to protect the network from such attacks.
Fabrication	Extremely high	Affects the authenticity of information. Hostile can inject false data and can destroy the authenticity of information.	Data authenticity can be applied to ensure that no information is changed during the transmission of data.
DoS	Extremely high	Malicious user may modify the packets or resend a packet again and again on network. User can also send bulk messages to devices in order to disturb the normal functionalities of devices.	Apply cryptographic techniques to ensure security of network. Apply authenticity to detect the malicious user and block them permanently. In this way, the network is prevented from damage.

Low-level attack: In this case, an attacker tries to attack a network and his attack is not successful.
Medium-level attack: In this attack, an attacker/intruder or an eavesdropper just listens to the medium but does not alter the integrity of data.
High-level attack: If an attack is carried on a network and it alters the integrity of data or modifies the data, it is called high-level attack.
Extremely high-level attack: In this case, an intruder/attacker attacks on a network by gaining unauthorized access and performing an illegal operation, making the network unavailable, sending bulk messages or jamming network.

1.6.3.1.4 False Data Injection Attacks An attacker who has hijacked the IoT device or node can inject false data into the system. When false data is sent to center and other IoT devices, it causes misbehavior. In addition, control data generated based on these false values also cause false control results.

1.6.3.2 Transport/Network Layer The function of this layer is to transfer the information collected by the perception layer to the information processing system through existing communication networks. In order to transfer information, the wireless and wired Internet networks are used. Therefore, all necessary care must be taken against hacker intrusion and illegal authorization. The related issues are discussed below.

1.6.3.2.1 Sybil Attack An attacker manipulates the node to present multiple identities for a single node due to which a considerable part of the system can be compromised resulting in false information about the redundancy.

1.6.3.2.2 Spoofing Attack In this type of attack, the attacker gains access to the IoT system and sends malicious data to the system. For spoofing attacks, we can give IP spoofing and RFID spoofing as examples. By obtaining the IP of an IoT device, an attacker can use this ID to send fake data to the system. Similarly, it can change the RFID tag and send fake data to the system.

1.6.3.2.3 Sinkhole Attack In a sinkhole attack, a compromised node or malicious node advertises fake rank information to form fake routes. After receiving the message packet, it drops the packet information. Sinkhole attacks affect the performance of IoT network protocols such as Routing Protocol (RPL)

1.6.3.2.4 Sleep Deprivation Attack Especially, nodes used in Wi-Fi networks are powered by batteries with a short lifetime. Therefore, the nodes that operate in sleep mode will be able to operate for a long time. By making constant requests, the attackers cause the node to be awake, thus quickly draining its battery and closing the node.

1.6.3.2.5 Denial-of-Service Attack   It is a busy attack by sending continuous requests to an IoT device. DoS attacks are performed in Ping of Death, Tear Drop, User Datagram Protocol (UDP) flood, Synchronize (SYN) flood and Layer 4 Denial of Service (LAND) attack type.

1.6.3.2.6 Malicious Code Injection   The attacker compromises a node to inject malicious code into the system, which could even result in a complete shutdown of the network, or in the worst case, the attacker can get a full control of the network.

1.6.3.2.7 Man-in-the-Middle Attack   A man-in-the-middle attack is a general term used when a perpetrator positions himself in a conversation between a user and an application, either to eavesdrop or to impersonate one of the parties, making it appear as if a normal exchange of information is underway. The goal of an attack is to steal login credentials.

1.6.3.3 Application Layer Challenges   The main function of the application layer is to analyze the information acquired from the transportation layer and process it. This layer guarantees the authenticity, integrity and confidentiality of the data [10, 9]. At this layer, we can get some important real-time. Challenges in the application layer of IoT are explained below.

1.6.3.3.1 Spear-Phishing Attack   An attacker can reap the ID and passwords by means of spoofing the authentication credentials of users via the inflamed e-mails and phishing websites.

1.6.3.3.2 Malicious Virus/Worm   An attacker can infect the IoT programs with malicious self-propagation attacks (worms, malicious program, etc.), after which he/she achieve or tamper with private data.

1.6.3.3.3 Sniffing Attack   An attacker can make an attack on an IoT device by introducing a sniffer utility into the device, which can benefit network facts resulting in corruption of the system.

1.6.3.3.4 Malicious Scripts   Malicious scripts constitute the scripts which can be introduced to the program, modified in a software program and deleted from software program with the motive of harming the device capabilities of IoT.

1.6.3.3.5 Denial-of-Service Attack   DoS attacks nowadays have become sophisticated; they offer a smoke screen to carry out attacks to breach the defensive system and hence data privacy of the user, while deceiving the victim into believing that the actual attack is happening somewhere else [9]. This puts the non-encrypted personal details of the user in the hands of the hacker.

D. E. Robles and R. J. Robles give the summary of security attacks in their paper [14], which is shown in Table 1.2. Table 1.3 is also taken from the same paper.

Table 1.2   IoT Security Attacks

PHYSICAL LAYER	NETWORK LAYER	APPLICATION LAYER
Eavesdropping	DoS attack	
RF jamming	Malicious code injection	
Spoofing	Sinkhole attack	Sniffing attack
Unauthorized access to the tags	Sybil attack	Spear-phishing attack
Tag cloning	Denial-of-sleep attack	
	Man-in-the-middle attack	

Table 1.3   IoT Attacks and Preventions/Solutions

LAYER	ATTACK/VULNERABILITY	SOLUTIONS
Physical layer	Eavesdropping	Apply encryption on all the devices that perform communication.
	RF jamming	RF jammer executes by entering jamming messages in the wireless network. Transmission of jamming messages can be prevented by cryptanalysis and steganography techniques.
	Spoofing	To avoid from spoofing and cloning attacks, apply identity-based authentication protocols. Physically unclonable function is a countermeasure for cloning attack.
	Unauthorized access to the tags	Tags can be protected from illegal access by unscrupulous readers through the authentication procedures of the APF systems.
	Tag cloning	To avoid from spoofing and cloning attacks, apply identity-based authentication protocols. Physically unclonable function is a countermeasure for cloning attack.

(Continued)

Table 1.3 (*Continued*) IoT Attacks and Preventions/Solutions

LAYER	ATTACK/VULNERABILITY		SOLUTIONS
Network layer	Sinkhole attack		Analyze data consistency and network flow information.
	Sybil attack		Use of artificial intelligence to recognize fake account patterns.
	Denial-of-sleep attack		Workload should be distributed among the components according to their capacity to avoid complete exhaustion of battery power.
	Man-in-the-middle attack		Apply data confidentiality and proper integration on data to ensure integrity. Encryption can also be applied so that no one can steal the information or modify the information or encode the information before transmission.
Application layer	DoS attack	Malicious code injection	Apply cryptographic techniques to ensure security of network.
			Apply authenticity to detect the malicious user and block them permanently. In this way, the network is prevented from damage.
	Sniffing attack		Connect to trusted networks. Encrypt all the traffic that leaves your system.
	Spear-phishing attack		Scan all inbound e-mail to spot indicators in the message header, domain information and message content that may indicate a message is suspicious.

References

1 Springer (2009).
2. Willke, T. L., Tientrakool, P., Maxemchuk, N. F.: Inter-Vehicle Communication (IVC) Protocol, IEEE XPlore, 02 June (2009).
3. Muntjir, M., Rahul, M., Alhumyani, H. A.: An Analysis of Internet of Things (IoT): Novel Architectures, Modern Applications, Security Aspects and Future Scope with Latest Case Studies IoT in Latest Trends, International Journal of Engineering Research & Technology (IJERT), Vol. 6, No. 06, June (2017).
4. Farooq, M. U., Waseem, M., Mazhar, S., Khairi A., Kamal, T.: A Review on Internet of Things (IoT), International Journal of Computer Applications (0975 8887), Vol. 113, No. 01, March (2015).
5. Patel, K. K., Patel, S. M.: Internet of Things-IOT: Definition, Characteristics, Architecture, Enabling Technologies, Application & Future Challenges, ISSN 2321 3361 © (2016) IJESC.
6. Polat, G., Sodah, F.: Security Issues in IoT: Challenges and Countermeasures, ISACA Istanbul Chapter, https://www.isaca-istanbul.org/security-issues-in-iot-challenges-and-countermeasures/[7.06.2020 14:22:47]

7. Lu, Y., Xu, L.: Internet of Things (IoT) Cybersecurity Research: A Review of Current Research Topics, IEEE Internet Of Things Journal, Vol. 6, No. 2, April (2019).

8. Madakam, S., Ramaswamy, R., Tripathi, S.: Internet of Things (IoT): A Literature Review, Journal of Computer and Communications, Vol. 3, 164–173, May (2015), http://www.scirp.org/journal/jcc

9. Mahmoud, R., Yousuf, T., Aloul, F., Zualkernan, I.: Internet of Things (IoT) Security: Current Status, Challenges and Prospective Measures, 10th International Conference for Internet Technology and Secured Transactions (ICITST), (2015), London.

10. Vashi, S., Ram, J., Modi, J., Verma, S., Prakash, C.: Internet of Things (IoT): A Vision, Architectural Elements, and Security Issues, International Conference on I-SMAC (IoT in Social, Mobile, Analytics and Cloud) (I-SMAC), (2017).

11. Alqassem, I., Svetinovic, D.: A Taxonomy of Security and Privacy Requirements for the Internet of Things (IoT), Proceedings of the 2014 IEEE IEEM, (2014).

12. Al-Garadi, M. A., Mohamed, A., Al-Ali, A. K., Du, X., Ali, I., Guizani, M.: A Survey of Machine and Deep Learning Methods, IEEE Communications Surveys & Tutorials, Vol. 22, No. 3, Third Quarter (2020).

13. Razzaq, M. A., Qureshi, M. A., Gill, S. H., Ullah, S.: Security Issues in the Internet of Things (IoT): A Comprehensive Study, (IJACSA) International Journal of Advanced Computer Science and Applications, Vol. 8, No. 6, (2017).

14. Robles, D. E., Robles, R. J.: State of Internet of Things (IoT) Security Attacks, Vulnerabilities and Solutions, Computer Reviews Journal Vol. 3, 2581–6640, (2019).

2

Robustness Analysis of PLC Programs with Respect to Sensor Interaction in IoT

MANALI CHAKRABORTY,
AGOSTINO CORTESI, PIETRO
FERRARA AND SARA FERRO

Università Ca' Foscari, Venezia VE, Italy

Contents

DOI: 10.1201/9781003149507-2

2.1 Introduction

A Programmable Logic Controller (PLC) is a fundamental component in an Industrial Control System (ICS). PLC is a control device used to automate industrial processes by collecting input data from field devices such as sensors, processing it and then sending commands to actuator devices such as motors. Being a pivotal device in ICS systems, PLCs are one of the preferred targets of cyber security attacks.

A PLC is a particular type of embedded device that is programed to manage and control physical components (motors, valves, sensors, etc.) based on system inputs and requirements. A PLC typically has three main components [2], namely: (i) An embedded operating system, (ii) a control system software and (iii) analog and digital inputs/ outputs (I/O). Hence, a PLC can be considered as a special digital computer executing specific instructions that collect data from input devices (e.g., sensors), send commands to output devices (e.g., actuators) and transmit data to a central operations center. PLCs are commonly found in Supervisory Control and Data Acquisition (SCADA) systems as field devices. Because they contain a programmable memory, PLCs a customizable control of physical components through a user programmable interface [4].

2.1.1 PLC & IoT

In the last decades, the main focus area in the PLC-related research was only concerned with the specification of the PLC application logic itself. On the other hand, networking, which was always a wired system, didn't extend beyond the factory floor. Now, with the advent of wireless industrial interfaces, low-cost sensors and cloud computing has given rise to a set of emerging requirements for industrial applications [1]. These PLC Internet of Things (IoT) applications center around sensor-based alerts in various mediums (email, SMS, push notifications), easy access to data on PC and mobile devices and increasingly sophisticated data analytics.

Consequently, programming a PLC application takes on a new meaning, with most of the impact manifesting not only in the core PLC code but also at the interfaces between the PLC and the other components that make IoT systems a reality. While integrating PLC codes in an IoT environment, the following issues become a challenge [3, 26]:

1. Data Acquisition: The manner in which a PLC exposes its I/O (sensors and actuators) to external hardware and software components is the primary determinant of much of the impact that will be on the PLC code. At one extreme, the code running on the PLC can be updated to make specific values available as outputs or to process new external inputs like remote control requests. At the other extreme, PLC's existing outputs can be further processed using a standard industrial communication protocol (e.g., Modbus) and base your IoT system requirements on what the PLC already exposes.

2. Communication Method: PLC communication interfaces can be either wired or wireless. Wired interfaces are by far the most common (e.g., serial cable), and in an IoT context, they imply the use of an internet-connected gateway that collects local PLC data via cable and transports to its final destination (e.g., a public or private cloud datastore).

3. Core behavior impact: PLCs are typically used for their hard real-time capabilities, and it is generally not advisable to introduce IoT functionality directly into their application logic. Any new system functionality that involves networking should be kept completely isolated from a PLC's core control loop. This applies to both local networking and especially to remote networking, with external network communication

being particularly unsuited to the involvement in driving the real-time controls due to its nondeterministic nature.

Leveraging a gateway-based architecture enables you to get the best of both the worlds, with PLCs continuing to take care of automated control tasks while sending their data into the IoT infrastructure via a standard communication protocol like Modbus.

4. Reusability: In order to get the maximum return on your PLC development effort, you should aim to build your system in a way that PLC vendor is independent, by adhering to standards as much as possible.

5. Security: Security is understandably a major concern when considering whether to extend a PLC-based system with IoT capabilities, particularly when external networks, e.g., the internet, are involved. To design your system to a proxy network activity via a secure, internet-connected gateway and to avoid connecting Modbus devices directly to the internet, you can achieve the benefits of IoT systems while mitigating the associated security risks.

There are many options available when it comes to combining PLCs and IoT technologies, all of which share the common goal of successfully merging the hard real-time guarantees and the rugged form factor of PLCs with the remote monitoring, alerting and advanced data analytics of the IoT.

2.1.2 Motivation

Robustness can be defined as the ability of a program to produce an "acceptable" output in spite of exceptional or erroneous inputs. Such a feature is particularly important for critical applications of the software whose execution environment cannot be fully foreseen at the time of development [17]. Besides that, there exist several systems where a PLC is highly interactive, thus input-dependent. In this case, in particular, the input is received from physical sensors. In such scenarios, the primary processing of the PLC is dependent on the input values. Robustness verification allows to detect the level of tolerance for input values that does not compromise the overall expected behavior.

2.1.3 Contribution

We provide a general methodology for automatic generation of Timed Automata (TA)–based models from the code written in Structured Control Language (SCL). The following are the specific contributions of this chapter:

1. We formalize the rules for expressing a PLC program written in SCL into a domain-specific language (DSL) using Xtext (open-source software framework for developing DSL).
2. We provide a set of transformation rules from DSL code to TA-based models.
3. Since generating a model for an entire PLC program tends to be large at size, we focus only on the sensor-provided inputs. We generate a TA model for each input, and we define the dependencies among them.
4. We feed the resulting automaton in a model checking system (UPPAAL) to verify robustness properties expressed as a temporal logic formulas in CTL.
5. We illustrate this approach step by step on a simple, real case study and discuss the scalability in more general settings.

2.1.4 Structure of the Chapter

The rest of the chapter is structured as follows: Section 2.2 discusses some relevant works in this domain, while the detailed methodology is described in Section 2.3. In Section 2.4, we formalize robustness properties and we describe how to verify them on a small yet complex example. Section 2.5 discusses some experimental results. Section 2.6 concludes.

2.2 Related Work

2.2.1 Vulnerabilities of PLC Programs

Generally, the attacks on PLC can be classified as access control attacks, firmware modification, control flow attacks, configuration modification, communication channel attacks, etc.

In the paper by Wang et al. [5], the authors proposed three different types of attacks on PLC registers: Replay attacks, man-in-the-middle attacks and S7 authentication bypass attacks. They explored the Siemens PLC's access control vulnerability by reading and writing the PLC's intermediate register data to achieve the effect of abnormal communications. In the PLC architecture, the CPUs store the results of the program into the intermediate registers and then execute them. Thus, rewriting the values of intermediate registers can affect the ongoing process in PLC. They attacked on the Siemens S7 series controllers, such as S7-200, S7-300, S7-400 and S7-1200.

In the paper by Wardak et al. [4], authors carried out a security analysis of the most common PLC access control mechanism, namely, password-based access control. They explained how passwords are stored in PLC memory, how they can be intercepted in the network, how they can be cracked, etc. As a consequence of these vulnerabilities, they could carry out advanced attacks on ICS system setup, such as replay, PLC memory corruption, etc.

Firmware alteration is another type of attack. Basnight et al. [6] performed an update on the version number of the PLC by exploiting the firmware. First, they searched the firmware for locations that referenced the version number. Then using reverse engineering, they inspected the disassembled information and modified the version number bytes appropriately. They also calculated the correct checksum values for modified data and updated in the new firmware binary file. The utility then validated the binary to confirm that the checksum values were updated correctly.

Another work on firmware modification is reported in the study by Garcia and Zonouz [7], where the authors implemented a stealthy attack on firmware by manipulating the I/O. The firmware acts at an intermediate level between the main control section of the PLC and the outer world. The inputs toward PLC's control logic passes through the firmware layer, as well as the outputs from the PLC. Thus, the attackers gain the insight knowledge of these communications, in particular, the PLC's control of I/O, and the connection between the firmware and control logic programs, by using reverse engineering to the PLC, and provide fake information to the outer world.

In the study by Abbasi and Hashemi [8], the authors performed another firmware modification attack by exploiting the shortcomings of the ICSs in the PLC security that did not consider the dynamic changes of memory contents as well as control flow. They developed a rootkit on the CODESYS PLC runtime to intercept I/O operations of the payload program. When the payload wants to read or write a certain I/O pin, at first, the interrupt handler installed by the attacker is performed, within which the attacker can reconfigure the I/O pins or modify the values to be read/written.

Firmware attacks typically require detailed knowledge on the target PLC's hardware components and reverse engineering of its firmware since PLCs are usually closed-source embedded devices [9]. An attacker needs to install the rootkit on PLCs either via the built-in remote firmware update mechanism or by loading it via JTAG interface [7]. For firmware update process protected by cryptographic means (e.g., certificate in the X.509 standard), it is hard to install a modified version of the firmware on the PLC. Alternatively, an attacker can load modified PLC firmware via JTAG interface. However, such an approach will require physical access to the PLC, possibly disassembling it.

In a recent work [10], authors proposed a runtime monitoring to develop runtime behavior models from the control system specifications to detect PLC payload attacks. Payload attacks are much easier to implement that firmware attack. It can be easily done if an attacker gains access to the PLC. The proposed solution in this paper can effectively detect the payload attacks. However, it suffers from memory overhead and execution time overhead.

In the study by Malchow et al. [11], a bump-in-the-wire device, called PLC guard, is introduced to intercept the communication between an engineering workstation and a PLC, allowing engineers to review the code and compare it against previous versions. Features of the PLC guard include various levels of graphical abstraction and summarization, which makes it easier to detect malicious code snippets.

In the study by Janicke et al. [12], an external runtime monitoring device (e.g., a computer or an Arduino microcontroller board) sits alongside the PLC, monitors its runtime behaviors (e.g., inputs, outputs, timers, counters) and verifies them against ICS specifications converted from a trusted version of the PLC payload program and written in interval temporal logic. It is shown that functional properties of payload program can be verified against ICS specifications, but the types of payload attacks that can be detected by this approach remain to be explored.

In the study by McLaughlin et al. [13] and Zonouz et al. [14], a trusted safety verifier is introduced as a bump-in-the-wire device that automatically analyzes the payload program that has to be downloaded onto a PLC and verifies whether critical safety properties are met using linear temporal logic (LTL). However, LTL implicitly assumes that the states of the systems are observed at the end of a set of time intervals. In the case of PLC payload program, snapshot of the states of system is taken at the end of each program scan cycle. As a result, the real-time properties that do not span multiple program scan cycles cannot be checked by the trusted safety verifier. For instance, a legitimate payload program is required to energize its output immediately when a certain input pin is energized. An attacker can inject malicious code and prolong the program scan cycle to cause a real-time property violation while evading code analytics based on the LTL.

A systematic static analysis approach to the detection of IoT vulnerabilities can be found in the study by Ferrara et al. [15], while in the study by Mandal et al. [16], a software analysis is devised that leverages an existing intra-program taint analysis to detect security vulnerabilities in multiple communicating programs.

2.2.2 Model Checking of PLC Programs

The recent advances in safety critical systems and the increasing complexity of safety parameters compel the researchers to pay more attention on the formalization and verification of PLC programs against various safety parameters before deploying the PLCs.

Soliman et al. [19] and Thramboulidis et al. [20] presented a model transformation process for IEC 61131-3 function block diagrams (FBD) to TA in UPPAAL for automated verification of safety parameters. They took the PLC Open XML specification of FBD and transformed to the UPPAAL-based XML format for TA.

Canet et al. [22] have developed a formal method to perform the verification of PLC programs written in the Instruction List (IL) language. This method consists in applying symbolic model checking techniques in the framework of PLC programs. The characteristic elements of their approach are the choice of a significant fragment of the IL language, allowing to write some simple programs; a sharp transition system-based operational semantics of this fragment; a coding of these transition systems into the input language of a model checker (like Cadence SMV); the use of the LTL to write behavioral properties. Although based on simple and well-known concepts, this approach allows to prove or reject, in a completely automated way, the correctness of IL programs of a nontrivial size. A similar study on the validation of PLC programs has already been presented for Ladder Diagrams (LD) programs in the study by Rossi et al. [23].

PLCVerif [21] is a tool for verifying PLC programs based on various model checking techniques. It uses three model checking tools: NuSMV, Theta and CBMC. Among these tools, CBMC is a bounded model checker for C and C++, and Theta is another model checking tool that has several extensions for various types of formalisms, and finally, NuSMV is a state transition–based model checking framework. PLCVerif is a complete tool to perform verification on PLC program written over several languages. Unfortunately, on our PLC sample code an internal error occurs in PLCVerif that makes impossible to compare the system w.r.t. accuracy and performance. The main contribution of our work with respect to PLCVerif is twofold: On one hand, we provide a formal correctness proof of the language translation and automaton generation, and on the other hand, we are able to take full advantage of the UPPAAL model checker which provides a more efficient interpretation of the real-time properties and synchronization of more than one automata through a shared channel with respect to NuSMV [28]. We made use of PLCVerif as a back-to-back testing workbench for evaluating our tool, but we observed that very often PLCVerif results into internal errors, while our tool is able to successfully complete the verification process.

2.3 Proposed Methodology

Given a program P, where Σ is the set of all program states, the semantics of P can be expressed as the (possibly infinite) set of its execution traces:

$$\bigcup\left\{\langle\delta_0^i,\ldots,\delta_n^i,\ldots\rangle : i \in I, \delta_b^i \in \Sigma\right\}$$

where I is the set of possible sensor-dependent input values, and δ_b^i is the bth program memory state of an execution trace having i as the input value.

We further assume that $\Sigma_E \subseteq \Sigma$ and $\Sigma_\Delta \subseteq \Sigma$, where Σ_Δ denotes the set of acceptable final states and Σ_E is the set of error states.

We also assume $I = I_A \cup I_U$, where I_A is the set of acceptable inputs and I_U is the set of unacceptable inputs, possibly due to an internal attack.

The robustness of program P can be formalized as follows:

if P runs with an unacceptable input $i \in I_U$, then considering the execution

$$P(i) = \langle \delta_0^i, \ldots, \delta_n^i, \ldots \rangle$$

1. Either $P(i)$ gets into Σ_E, i.e., $\exists k \geq 0 : \delta_k^i \in \Sigma_E$, raising a detectable error state.

   or,

2. $P(i)$ is finite, its last element belongs to Σ_Δ, and it yields to an output value τ, which is anyway acceptable to the user, i.e., the presence of an erroneous input has marginal effect on the overall execution.

2.3.1 Methodology Overview

The crucial step for verifying PLC code written in the programming language SCL is to soundly translate it into a TA and apply that on a model checker tool like UPPAAL.

For our experiments, we chose UPPAAL because it supports various features of model checkers, but other model checkers (e.g., DREAM, TAPAAL or BLAST) might have been adopted as well.

Figure 2.1 depicts the overall architecture of our robustness verifier. The following are the main contributions:

- **A theoretical framework for generating models out of SCL code,** which includes
  - Defining concrete semantics for both SCL and TA
  - Provide the formal definition of the translation rules
  - Provide their formal proofs of correctness
- **Implementation of the framework,** i.e.,
  - Translation of SCL programs in a DSL using Xtext

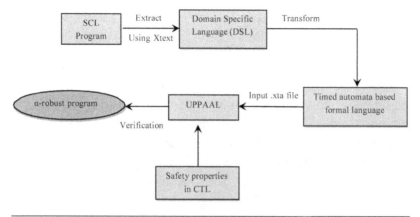

Figure 2.1   Proposed framework for robustness checking.

- Generation of TA-based models from that DSL to feed UPPAAL. This process can be executed with the help of Accelio
- Applying the UPPAAL model checker for finalizing the robustness verification

2.3.2 *Syntax and Semantics of SCL*

The starting point is SCL, i.e., a high-level textual programming language [25]. A program in SCL can call programs in other PLC languages, and programs written in other PLC languages can call programs in SCL. SCL can be structured as a sequence of various blocks, such as:

- Organization blocks (OB): They determine the structure of the program. The OB for normal program execution on PLCs is determined in OB. This block determines the cyclic semantics of the PLCs, and it represents the interface between the main system and PLC.
- Function blocks (FB): They are functions which can also store data between function calls; they can be called by OB and other FBs. They have internal memory.
- Functions (FC): They correspond to mainstream programming language functions; they can be called as OB and FB with their parameters and have no memory state.
- Data blocks (DB): They are used for storing and sharing data, helping to store user data.

- User-defined data types (UDT): They are used to define complex data types and used for storing UDT.

In addition to high-level language elements, SCL also includes language elements typical of PLCs such as inputs, outputs, timers, bit memory, block calls, etc. In other words, SCL complements and extends the STEP 7 programming software and its programming languages Ladder Logic and Statement List [24].

The programs we use in the experiments start with an FB, to which we will refer as the main FB. The programs can have calls to other FBs, functions, DBs and data types.

All functions and FBs in SCL can have variables of different types. Input variables get values from the calling block. For the topmost FB, the input variables get values from the input ports. Output variables are used to return values to the calling block. For the topmost FB, the output variables contain the values that are sent to the output ports. In-output variables are a combination of input variables and output variables, and these variables get values from the calling block, or input ports, and return values to the calling block or send them to the output ports. Static variables can be used within the blocks. FBs have memory; therefore, they can keep the values of static variables after the program has returned to the calling block. This also makes it possible for these variables to have an initial value. A function has no memory; therefore, static variables in a function have no initial values and do not keep their values after the program has returned to the calling block.

SCL uses control statements to take care of selective instructions and repetition instructions. The control statements we use are IF, ELSEIF, ELSE and WHILE. SCL also supports case distinction, loops and jump statements. For conditional expressions, the standard Boolean operators can be used.

The predefined data types we use are BOOL, INT, UINT, WORD, ARRAY, STRUCT, TIME and REAL. Other predefined data types are dates, chars, timers and doubles. The data types ARRAY and STRUCT do not have a specified size because the size varies per specification.

2.3.2.1 Syntax of SCL According to the IEC-61131-3 standard [27], every PLC program consists of one or many Programming Organization Unit (POUs). These POUs are the smallest executable units of each PLC program and can be of several types (as termed by the SIEMENS Simatic-STEP7): OB, FB, function, DB and UDT.

An SCL program can be defined as a list of *statements*, and each *statement* can be defined as a collection of *keywords* and *expressions*, terminating by a ";".

While *statements* are the basic elements of an SCL program, a *block* is a basic executable unit in an SCL program. In this paper, we generate a TA-based model for each block of an SCL program. Now, we define the semantics of a simple block for a program written in SCL.

Generally, the *statements* within a *block* can be roughly categorized in five sections as:

- Block start statements: The start statements consist of a unique *keyword* for each type of blocks following by the name of that block.
- Block attribute statements: Attribute statements can be of two types: Block attributes and system attributes for blocks.
- Declaration statements: The declaration section must contain all specifications required to create the bases for the code section, for example, definition of constants and declaration of variables and parameters.
- Code statements: The code section is introduced by the *keyword* BEGIN and terminated with END_*, where "*" represents the type of that particular block.
- Block end statements: It is similar to the start statements, but it has only keywords for each block.

The syntax of SCL, according to IEC 61131-3, is depicted in Figure 2.2, while the semantics is formalized in Figure 2.3.

2.3.3 Syntax and Semantics of TA

A TA [18] is essentially a finite automaton (i.e., a graph containing a finite set of nodes or locations and a finite set of labeled edges) extended with real-valued variables. Such an automaton may be considered as an abstract model of a timed system. The variables model the logical clocks in the system, which are initialized with zero when the system is started, and then increase synchronously with the same rate. Clock constraints, i.e., guards on edges, are used to restrict the behavior of the automaton. A transition represented by an edge can be taken when the clock values satisfy the guard labeled on the edge. Clocks may be reset to zero when there is a transition.

kwords ∈ Keywords
Keywords = {BEGIN, FUNCTION, FUNCTION BLOCK, ORGANIZATION BLOCK, DATA BLOCK, END_FUNCTION, END_FUNCTION_BLOCK, END_ORGANIZATION_BLOCK, END_DATA BLOCK, VAR, VAR TEMP, VAR IN OUT, VAR INPUT, VAR OUTPUT}

$x, y \in$ GVar (global variables)
$u, v \in$ LVar (local variables)
$n \in$ Num (numbers)
$t \in$ Type (datatype of variables)
$l \in$ Lab (labels)

$a \in Exp_A$
$b \in Exp_B$
$S \in$ stat

$op_A \in A_{op}$ Arithmetic operator
$A_{op} = \{+, -, *, \%, /\}$
$op_B \in B_{op}$ Boolean operator
$B_{op} = \{AND, OR, XOR, NOR\}$
$op_R \in R_{op}$ Relational operator
$R_{op} = \{\leq, <, >, \geq, =, /=\}$

$a ::= x|n|a_1 \; A_{op} \; a_2$
$b ::= x|n|true|false|b_1 \; B_{op} \; b_2|a_1 \; R_{op} \; a_2| \; not \; b$

$S ::= x := a|$
$S_1 ; S_2|$
if [b] **then** S_1 **else** $S_2|$
while [b] **do** S

Figure 2.2   SCL syntax.

2.3.3.1 Syntax of TA   In order to define the syntax of TA, we define the following notation:

$x_t, \; y_t \in$ Var (timed variables)
$m, n \in$ Par (parameters)
$t \in$ Clk (clock)
$n \in$ Num (numbers)
Γ is the environment mapping from variables to numbers
$g \in G$ (set of guards or clock constraints)
$g ::= x_t \;|true| \; false| \; x_t \; R_{op} \; x_t$ (guard)
$a, z \in \Delta$ (set of actions)
$a ::= s := y$ (assign)
$y ::= x_t \; |n \; | \; x_t \; A_{op} \; x_t$ (assign)
$z ::= x_t \; |n \; | \; ! \; |? \; | \; |true| \; false| \; x_t \; R_{op} \; x_t \; | \; x_t \; R_{op} \; n$ (sync)
$A_{op} = \{+, \; -, \; *, \; \%, \; /\}$
$R_{op} = \{\leq, \; <, \; >, \; \geq, \; =, \; \neq\}$

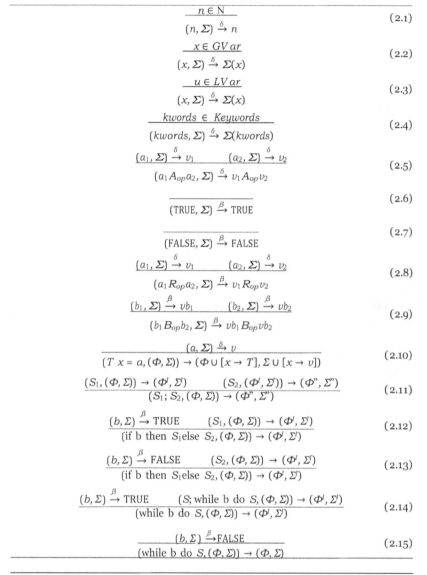

$$\frac{n \in N}{(n, \Sigma) \xrightarrow{\delta} n} \tag{2.1}$$

$$\frac{x \in GVar}{(x, \Sigma) \xrightarrow{\delta} \Sigma(x)} \tag{2.2}$$

$$\frac{u \in LVar}{(x, \Sigma) \xrightarrow{\delta} \Sigma(x)} \tag{2.3}$$

$$\frac{kwords \in Keywords}{(kwords, \Sigma) \xrightarrow{\delta} \Sigma(kwords)} \tag{2.4}$$

$$\frac{(a_1, \Sigma) \xrightarrow{\delta} v_1 \qquad (a_2, \Sigma) \xrightarrow{\delta} v_2}{(a_1 A_{op} a_2, \Sigma) \xrightarrow{\delta} v_1 A_{op} v_2} \tag{2.5}$$

$$\frac{}{(TRUE, \Sigma) \xrightarrow{\beta} TRUE} \tag{2.6}$$

$$\frac{}{(FALSE, \Sigma) \xrightarrow{\beta} FALSE} \tag{2.7}$$

$$\frac{(a_1, \Sigma) \xrightarrow{\delta} v_1 \qquad (a_2, \Sigma) \xrightarrow{\delta} v_2}{(a_1 R_{op} a_2, \Sigma) \xrightarrow{\beta} v_1 R_{op} v_2} \tag{2.8}$$

$$\frac{(b_1, \Sigma) \xrightarrow{\beta} vb_1 \qquad (b_2, \Sigma) \xrightarrow{\beta} vb_2}{(b_1 B_{op} b_2, \Sigma) \xrightarrow{\beta} vb_1 B_{op} vb_2} \tag{2.9}$$

$$\frac{(a, \Sigma) \xrightarrow{\delta} v}{(T\ x = a, (\Phi, \Sigma)) \to (\Phi \cup [x \to T], \Sigma \cup [x \to v])} \tag{2.10}$$

$$\frac{(S_1, (\Phi, \Sigma)) \to (\Phi', \Sigma') \qquad (S_2, (\Phi', \Sigma')) \to (\Phi'', \Sigma'')}{(S_1; S_2, (\Phi, \Sigma)) \to (\Phi'', \Sigma'')} \tag{2.11}$$

$$\frac{(b, \Sigma) \xrightarrow{\beta} TRUE \qquad (S_1, (\Phi, \Sigma)) \to (\Phi', \Sigma')}{(if\ b\ then\ S_1 else\ S_2, (\Phi, \Sigma)) \to (\Phi', \Sigma')} \tag{2.12}$$

$$\frac{(b, \Sigma) \xrightarrow{\beta} FALSE \qquad (S_2, (\Phi, \Sigma)) \to (\Phi', \Sigma')}{(if\ b\ then\ S_1 else\ S_2, (\Phi, \Sigma)) \to (\Phi', \Sigma')} \tag{2.13}$$

$$\frac{(b, \Sigma) \xrightarrow{\beta} TRUE \qquad (S; while\ b\ do\ S, (\Phi, \Sigma)) \to (\Phi', \Sigma')}{(while\ b\ do\ S, (\Phi, \Sigma)) \to (\Phi', \Sigma')} \tag{2.14}$$

$$\frac{(b, \Sigma) \xrightarrow{\beta} FALSE}{(while\ b\ do\ S, (\Phi, \Sigma)) \to (\Phi, \Sigma)} \tag{2.15}$$

Figure 2.3   SCL semantics.

Then, a TA can be defined as a tuple (L, l_0, E, S), where

- L is a finite set of locations (or nodes)
- $l_0 \in L$ is the initial location
- $E \subseteq \langle L \times G \times \Delta \times L \rangle$ is the set of edges
- S: Var $\to$ Clk $\to$ Num, set of states, that returns the values of variable at a particular time

The semantics of a TA is defined as a transition system where a state or configuration is a pair of the current location and the current values of variables at that time, i.e., $\langle l, S \rangle$.

There are two types of transitions between states. The automaton may either delay for some time (a delay transition) or follow an enabled edge (an action transition).

The transitions are formalized as:

$$\frac{n \in \mathrm{N}}{\langle n, \Gamma \rangle \xrightarrow{\tau} n} \tag{2.16}$$

$$\frac{x \in Var}{\langle x, \Gamma \rangle \xrightarrow{\tau} \Gamma(x)} \tag{2.17}$$

$$\frac{m \in Par}{\langle m, \Gamma \rangle \xrightarrow{\tau} \Gamma(m)} \tag{2.18}$$

$$\frac{\langle x_1, \Gamma \rangle \xrightarrow{\tau} u_1 \qquad \langle x_2, \Gamma \rangle \xrightarrow{\tau} u_2}{\langle x_1 A_{op} x_2, \Gamma \rangle \xrightarrow{\psi} u_1 A_{op} u_2} \tag{2.19}$$

$$\frac{\langle x_1, \Gamma \rangle \xrightarrow{\tau} u_1 \qquad \langle x_2, \Gamma \rangle \xrightarrow{\tau} u_2}{\langle x_1 R_{op} x_2, \Gamma \rangle \xrightarrow{\tau} u_1 R_{op} u_2} \tag{2.20}$$

$$\frac{x \in Var, t \in Clk}{\langle x, t, s \rangle \xrightarrow{\alpha} s(x_t)} \tag{2.21}$$

$$\frac{\langle l, g, \delta, l' \rangle \in E, s(g_t) = true, s' = s(\delta_{t+1})}{\langle l, s, t \rangle \rightarrow \langle l', s' \rangle} \tag{2.22}$$

$\langle l, s, t \rangle$ is the current location and state of a TA at time t, and if the guard conditions are true, i.e., if $g_t = true$ at time t, then the transition will be made at $\langle l', s' \rangle$. Also, for this transition, the action can be either a(assign) or z(sync) or both.

$$\frac{\exists \langle l, g, \Delta, l' \rangle \in E}{s(g, t) \rightarrow true} \qquad \frac{\nexists \langle l, g, \Delta, l' \rangle \in E}{s(g_t) \rightarrow false} \tag{2.23}$$

The value of $s(g_t)$ is true, if there exists an edge between l and l', at time t. Otherwise $s(g_t)$ is false.

$$\frac{s(g_t)=true}{\langle s(g_t),t+1,s\rangle\overset{f}{\rightarrow}s(g_{t+1})} \tag{2.24}$$

$$\frac{\delta\in\Delta}{\langle s(\delta_t),t+1,s\rangle\overset{f}{\rightarrow}s(\delta_{t+1})} \tag{2.25}$$

$$\frac{s(g_t)=false,s'=s(\delta_{t+1})}{\langle l,s,t\rangle\rightarrow\langle l,s',t+1\rangle} \tag{2.26}$$

While the guard is not satisfied for an edge, the TA stays in the same location l. However, the state s will change from s to s', where $s'(\delta_{t+1})=s(s(\delta_t),t+1)$

2.3.4 Transforming SCL to TA

The transformation function [27] considers one statement of an SCL program at a time and produces its corresponding transition in a TA model. As we already described earlier, a TA can be described as a 4-tuple $\langle L,l_0,E,S\rangle$. We can represent the transformation between SCL programs into TA models using the function $\Pi:\langle inst_{SCL},A,l_{in}\rangle\rightarrow\langle A',l_{fin}\rangle$, where $inst_{SCL}$ is the set of statements for SCL, and A is the TA corresponding to the SCL program, and l_{fin} is the final location or ending node of the TA.

The Π function considers change of states during the execution of SCL program and maps it to its corresponding equivalent transition in the TA model.

Now, A can be represented as a 4-tuple $\langle L,l_0,E,S\rangle$, where L is the set of nodes or locations in the TA, $l_0\in L$ denotes the starting node of the TA, E is the set of edges, that can further be described as $\langle L\times G\times\Delta\times L\rangle$, $e\in E=(l,g,\delta,l')$, where e is an edge or transition in TA from current location l to next location l', with guard g and actions δ.

Given a TA A, the transformation rules from an SCL statement to a corresponding TA transition can be described as:

$$\Pi\langle inst_{SCL},A,l_{in}\rangle\rightarrow\langle A',l_{fin}\rangle.$$

Now, the TA model starts at the *BEGIN* keyword in the SCL program. The variable declaration parts are then added in the corresponding *.xta* file. The local variables that are declared in the time of function declaration are mapped as parameters in the UPPAAL model.

Hence, at the beginning, when the automaton is empty, $A = \left(L = \{\emptyset\}, l_0 = \varepsilon, E = \{\emptyset\}, S \right)$. The translation rules are described below:

$$\Pi \langle BEGIN, \varepsilon, \varepsilon \rangle \to \left\langle L \cup \left\{ l_{fin} = new(node) \right\}, l_0 = l_{fin}, \{\emptyset\}, S, l_{fin} \right\rangle \quad (2.27)$$

$$\Pi \langle END\_FUNCTION\_BLOCK, A, l_{fin} \rangle \to \langle A, l_{fin} \rangle \quad (2.28)$$

$$\Pi \langle END\_ORGANIZATION\_BLOCK, A, l_{fin} \rangle \to \langle A, l_{fin} \rangle \quad (2.29)$$

$$\Pi \langle END\_FUNCTION, A, l_{fin} \rangle \to \langle A, l_{fin} \rangle \quad (2.30)$$

$$\Pi \langle END\_DATA\_BLOCK, A, l_{fin} \rangle \to \langle A, l_{fin} \rangle \quad (2.31)$$

$$\Pi \langle x := a, A, l_{in} \rangle \to \left\langle L \cup \left\{ l_{fin} = new(node) \right\}, l_0, E \cup \right.$$

$$\left. \left\{ \left(l_{in}, TRUE, x := a, l_{fin} \right) \right\}, S, l_{fin} \right\rangle \quad (2.32)$$

$$\frac{\Pi \langle stat_1, A, l_{in} \rangle \to \left\langle A', l_{fin} = new(node) \right\rangle}{\langle stat_1, stat_2, A, l_{in} \rangle \to \left\langle L \cup \left\{ \left(l_{fin}, l'_{fin} \right) \right\}, l_0, E \cup E', S \cup S', l'_{fin} \right\rangle} \quad (2.33)$$

$$\Pi \langle (\text{IF } b \text{ THEN } stat_1 \text{ ELSE } stat_2 \text{ ENDIF}), A, l_{in} \rangle \to$$

$$\left\langle L \cup \left\{ l_1 = new(node), l_2 = new(node), l_{fin} = new(node) \right\}, \right.$$

$$E \cup \left\{ \left(l_{in}, b := = TRUE, stat_1, l_1 \right), \left(l_{in}, b := = FALSE, stat_2, l_2 \right), \right.$$

$$\left. \left(l_1, TRUE, \epsilon, l_{fin} \right), \left(l_2, TRUE, \epsilon, l_{fin} \right) \right), S \cup \left\{ S[l_1], S[l_2] \right\}, l_{fin} \right\} \right\rangle$$

$$(2.34)$$

Figure 2.4 x: = a.

$$\Pi\langle(\text{WHILE b DO stat}), A, l_{in}\rangle \rightarrow \langle L \cup \{(l_1 = new(node),$$

$$l_{fin} = new(node))\}, l_0, E \cup \{(l_{in}, b: == TRUE, \epsilon, l_1),$$

$$(l_{in}, b: == FALSE, \epsilon, l_{fin})(l_1, TRUE, stat, l_{in})\}, S \cup \{S[l_1]\}, l_{fin}\rangle$$

$$(2.35)$$

For instance, by applying the transformation rules in Figures 2.4–2.6, the SCL code depicted in Figure 2.7 will result in the TA depicted in Figure 2.8.

2.3.5 Transformation Rules Correctness

In this section, we prove the correctness of the transformation function Π introduced in Section 2.3.4. The transformation function $\Pi\langle inst_{SCL}, A, l_{in}\rangle \rightarrow \langle A', l_{fin}\rangle$ takes an SCL instruction $inst_{SCL}$ and a TA model A, with the entry location point l_{in} and produces a modified TA model A', where l_{fin} is the exit location point.

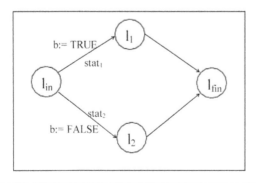

Figure 2.5   IF b THEN stat₁ ELSE stat₂ ENDIF.

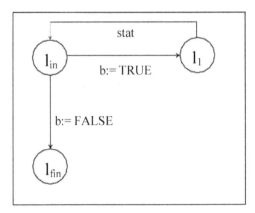

Figure 2.6 WHILE b DO stat.

In an SCL program, trace is (possibly infinite) a list of states and statements starting from the initial state $S_0 = \emptyset : \langle S_0, stm_1, S_1, \ldots, S_{n-1}, stm_n, S_n, \ldots \rangle$.

In a TA, a path is a sequence of nodes (with a corresponding state) and edges starting at the initial node $l_0 : \langle l_0 S_0', e_1, l_1 S_1', e_2, \ldots, l_m S_m', \ldots \rangle$;

```
FUNCTION_BLOCK Test

VAR_INPUT
        x : INT;
        y : INT;
END_VAR

VAR_OUTPUT
        out : INT;
END_VAR

BEGIN
        out := 0;
        IF x > y THEN
                out := x/y;
        ELSE
                out := y/x;
        END_IF;

END_FUNCTION_BLOCK
```

Figure 2.7 A small SCL code.

SCL instructions	Transformation Rules	TA Model
BEGIN	$\Pi \langle BEGIN, \varepsilon, \varepsilon \rangle \to \langle l_0, l_0, \{\emptyset\}, S, l_0 \rangle$	l0
out := 0;	$\Pi \langle out := 0, \langle l_0, l_0, \emptyset, S, l_0 \rangle, l_0 \rangle \to$ $\langle \{l_0, l_1\}, l_0, \{l_0, TRUE, out := 0, l_1\}, S, l_1 \rangle$	l0 →(out:=0)→ l1
IF x > y THEN $\quad$ out := x/y; ELSE $\quad$ out := y/x; END_IF;	$\Pi \langle IF\ x > y\ THEN\ out := x/y;$ $ELSE\ out := y/x;\ END\_IF; \langle \{l_0, l_1\},$ $l_0, \{l_0, TRUE, out := 0, l_1\}, S, l_1 \rangle, l_1 \rangle$ $\to \langle \{l_0, l_1, l_2, l_3, l_4\}, l_0, \{(l_0, TRUE,$ $out := 0, l_1), (l_1, (x > y) == TRUE,$ $out := x/y, l_2), (l_1, (x > y) == FALSE,$ $out := y/x, l_3), (l_2, TRUE, \varepsilon, l_4),$ $(l_3, TRUE, \varepsilon, l_4)\}, S, l_4 \rangle$	l0 →(out:=0)→ l1, x>y out:=x/y, x<=y out:=y/x, l2, l3, l4

Figure 2.8 Example of the proposed transformation method.

we go from one node to another by traversing an edge with associated constraints and actions.

In SCL, variables are split into I/O variables. This corresponds in the TA just to add to the initial state of all the variables. The state of the output of the program corresponds to the state of the corresponding variables in the final state at the end of execution in the automaton. So, when we get to the final node in the automaton, we just project the state over the output variables.

We aim to prove that given any initial trace segment $\langle S_0, stm_1, S_1, \ldots, S_{n-1}, stm_n, S_n \rangle$, there is a corresponding path $\langle l_0 S_0', e_1, l_1 S_1', \ldots, l_{in} S_{in}', e', l_{fin} S_{fin}' \rangle$ such that if we assume that after traversing the path $\langle l_0 S_0', e_1, l_1 S_1', \ldots, l_{in} S_{in}' \rangle$ we get to a state $S_{in}' = S_{n-1}$, then there is a path $\langle l_{in} S_{in}', \ldots, l_{fin} S_{fin}' \rangle$ such that the final state $S_{fin}' = S_n$.

The proof is by structural induction, by considering the different types of statements and by the corresponding transformation rules.

2.3.5.1 Basic Case: Begin At the beginning of the SCL program, the BEGIN statement is executed, where the state of variables is empty. In correspondence to the trace $\langle S_0 = \emptyset, BEGIN, S_0 \rangle$, we can easily recognize the empty path $\langle l_0, \emptyset \rangle$ in the automaton.

2.3.5.2 Assignment   If the last statement of the SLC trace is an assignment $x: = a$, the SCL semantics rule (2.10) applies:

$$\frac{\langle a, S_{n-1}\rangle \overset{\delta}{\to} v}{\langle T\,x = a,(\Phi, S_n)\rangle \to (\Phi \cup [x \to T], S_{n-1} \cup [x \to v])}.$$

By the transformation rule of the assignment (2.32), a node l_{fin} and an edge e' were introduced in the automaton, with an action on the edge e' that corresponds to the assignment of value a to x.

Let us consider the path $\langle (l_{in}S'_{in}), e', (l_{fin}S'_{fin})\rangle$ in the automaton. By applying the rules (2.21, 2.22 and 2.25) of the TA semantics, in S'_{fin} the values of the variables different from x are the same as in S'_{in}, whereas the value of x is $S'_{in}(a)$. Then, $S'_{fin} = S_n$ as desired.

2.3.5.3 Conditional Statement   If the statement is "IF b THEN $stat_1$ ELSE $stat_2$" and in S_{n-1} the condition b is true, by the SCL semantic rule (2.12), we have

$$\frac{\langle b, S_{n-1}\rangle \overset{\beta}{\to} \text{TRUE} \quad \langle stat_1, (\Phi, S_{n-1})\rangle \to (\Phi', S_n)}{\langle \text{if b then } stat_1 \text{ else } stat_2, (\Phi, S_{n-1})\rangle \to (\Phi', S_n)},$$

and we know that S_n is the result of the application of the statement $stat_1$.

Recall from the translation rule (2.34) of the "if then else" statement, that three nodes and four edges were introduced in the automaton. As we assume that S'_{in} is equal to S_{n-1}, then in S'_{in} b is true.

Consider the following path in the automaton: $\langle (l_{in}S'_{in}), e'_1, (l_1 S'_{l_1}), e''_1, (l_{fin}S'_{fin})\rangle$. By applying the rules (2.22 and 2.24) of the TA semantics, we have that S'_{l_1} is equal to S_n, and as e''_1 doesn't make any action, S'_{fin} is equal to S'_{l_1}. Thus, $S'_{fin} = S_n$, as desired.

The proof in the case of b being false is similar.

2.3.5.4 While Loop Statement   If the statement is "WHILE b DO stm," by the SCL semantics rules (2.14) and (2.15), we have

$$\frac{\langle b, S_{n-1}\rangle \overset{\beta}{\to} \text{TRUE} \quad \langle stm; \text{while b do } stm, (\Phi, S_{n-1})\rangle \to (\Phi', S_n)}{\langle \text{while b do } stm, (\Phi, S_{n-1})\rangle \to (\Phi', S_n)}$$

$$\frac{\langle b, S_{n-1}\rangle \xrightarrow{\beta} \text{FALSE}}{\langle \text{while b do } stm, (\Phi, S_{n-1})\rangle \to (\Phi, S_{n-1})}.$$

By the semantics of SCL, if the evaluation of b in S_{n-1} is false, we know that we do not enter into the while loop, and no change occurs in the variables state, so S_n is equal to S_{n-1}. Otherwise, if b is true in S_{n-1}, then S_n is obtained by applying the statement stm and then calling the while statement again.

By the transformation rule (2.35) of the while statement, two nodes and three edges were introduced in the automaton. If in the SCL trace b is false in state S_{n-1}, by inductive hypothesis, S'_{in} is equal to S_{n-1}, and then in S'_{in}, the condition b is false too. In the automaton, we consider the path $\langle (l_{in}S'_{in}), e'', (l_{fin}S'_{fin})\rangle$. In other words on the SCL side when b is false, we exit the while, and this corresponds in the TA to move to the final node l_{fin} by the edge e'' that has no action. By applying the rule (2.26) of the TA semantics, we have that S'_{fin} is equal to S'_{in}, so $S'_{fin} = S_{n-1}$ and we know that $S_{n-1} = S_n$, so $S'_{fin} = S_n$ as required.

Now consider the other case, when in the SCL state S_{n-1} b is true. By inductive hypothesis, S'_{in} is equal to S_{n-1}, where b is also true. Let us assume that in the SCL program, we iterate the while loop m times, where m can be finite or infinite, this corresponds in the TA to cross the path:
$$\langle (l_{in}S'_k), e', (l_1S'_k), e'_1, (l_{in}S'_{k+1}), e', (l_1S'_{k+1}), e'_1, (l_{in}S'_{k+2}), \ldots, l_{in}S'_{k+m-1}, e'_{m-1}, (l_{in}S'_{k+m})\rangle.$$

At the mth iteration, by inductive hypothesis, the parallelism among what happens in the while loop in the SCL and what happens in the three states corresponding to the three nodes in the automaton is maintained. The path $\langle (l_{in}S'_k), e', (l_1S'_k), e'_1, (l_{in}S'_{k+1}), e', (l_1S'_{k+1}), e'_1, (l_{in}S'_{k+2}), \ldots\rangle$ corresponds to the iteration of the body of the while loop in the SCL program.

Focusing on the last iteration of the while in the SCL program, in the TA this corresponds to the path $\langle (l_{in}S'_{m-1}), e', (l_1S'_{m-1}), e'_1, (l_{in}S'_m), e'', (l_{fin}S'_{fin})\rangle$. By applying the rules (2.22 and 2.24) of the TA semantics, S'_{in} is updated to S'_{m-1}, and crossing the edge e'_1, makes S'_m equal to the effect of applying stm. Therefore, S'_m after the statement stm is equal to S_n. As $S'_{fin} = S'_{in} = S'_m$, we get $S'_{fin} = S_n$ as desired.

2.3.5.5 Ending Statement   As the END statement does not have any impact on the variables state, it corresponds to an empty transition applied to the final state of the TA.

2.4 Robustness Analysis

Given a TA that represents an SCL program, we may verify now robustness properties by using a model checker like UPPAAL. The temporal query language consists of state formulas and path formulas. A state formula is an expression that can be evaluated for a particular state in order to check a property (e.g., a deadlock), without looking at the behavior of the model. Path formula quantify over paths of execution and ask whether a given state formula p can be satisfied in any or all the states along any or all the paths [18]. We can identify three types of path formulas (path properties):

- Reachability properties ($E <> p$) are the simplest ones; they ask whether a given state formula, p, possibly can be satisfied by any reachable state.
  $E <> p$ = "there exist a path where p eventually holds".
- Safety properties ($E[]p$ and $A[]p$) are of the form: Something good is invariantly true. $E[]p$ = "there exists a path where p always holds";
  $A[]p$ = "for all paths p always holds".
- Liveness properties ($A <> p$ and $p --> q$) are of the form: Something good will eventually happen.
  $A <> p$ = for all paths p will eventually hold;
     $p --> q$ = whenever p holds, q will eventually hold.

We can express one property in terms of another one:

- $A[]p$ = not $E <>$ not p
- $A <> p$ = not $E[]$ not p
- $p --> q = A[](p$ imply $A <> q)$

As we already mentioned in the problem statement, let Σ_A be the set of acceptable final states and Σ_E be the set of erroneous states, and let I_A be the set of acceptable inputs and I_U be the set of unacceptable inputs. Then, as we are trying to verify the robustness of our program, two things are particularly relevant:

- The program will always lead to a correct output state for a valid input: $A[]\Sigma_A (I_A)$

- The program will never lead to a correct output state for an erroneous input, and it means that the program will always lead to an erroneous output for an erroneous input: $A[]\Sigma_E(I_U)$.

2.4.1 Bolts and Nuts Case Study

The case study that we consider consists of an automated line for boxing of bolts and nuts, managed by a PLC. We have chosen this example because it is highly interactive and input-dependent (see Figure 2.10).

We can see that in Figure 2.9, the machine starts working only if the key is inserted, then an external device can choose if it wants only bolts, only nuts or both bolts and nuts. In the machine, there are some

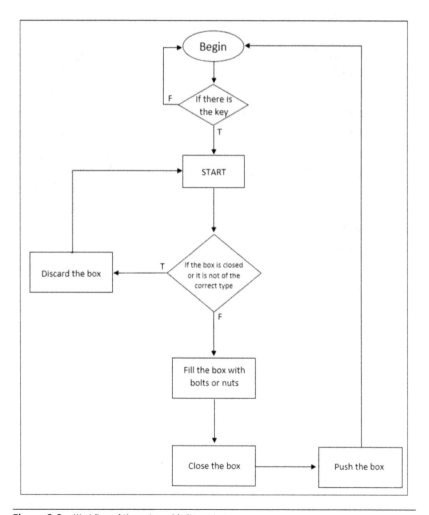

Figure 2.9 Workflow of the nuts and bolts system.

sensors and cameras that permit to understand if a box should be discarded and also where the box should be placed. So, for example, if the box is closed or it is not of the correct type (it means that if we want only bolts or only nuts, then we need a box with no partition, whereas if we want both bolts and nuts, then we need a bipartitioned box), then it is discarded. Otherwise, if there is the correct type of box and it is open, then the external device can now choose the number of pieces that it desires. The system checks if there are still pieces of bolts and nuts into the smaller conveyors, if there are not, then the machine stops working until there are new pieces. The box is filled with bolts or nuts or both, and the main conveyor starts again, so that the box goes on, the machine closes the box and pushes the box, and in this way, we can separate the boxes that are discarded from those that inside them contain pieces of bolts and nuts.

The complete PLC program source can be found in Appendix A. After generating the corresponding .xta file, we automatically create the TA depicted in Appendix B. By using UPPAAL, we can check some robustness properties. Unfortunately, "Out of memory" errors occur as there is a limit in the UPPAAL tool that allows the usage of memory until 2 GB only. This limit can be faced by splitting the model into subsystems, by using usual specialization techniques.

Our model will always get to a state where the box is discarded or contains bolts and nuts, so the system never stops because once the box is discarded, the process "restart" and the model already have the previous choice of bolts or nuts or both in the memory.

We can get stuck when we remain in the loops that recharge the conveyors of nuts and bolts because if no one recharges the conveyors with new pieces, then the machine stops until the box is filled with new pieces. Also in this case, we can say that our model is robust because if there are no more pieces, then the system stops until there are more pieces and if the machine goes on anyway when there are no more pieces, at the end in the box, there will not be the correct number of nuts or bolts. We are able to prove that the system is robust because when it receives correct inputs (given a choice there is the correct box opened), the machine works correctly, and also when it receives erroneous inputs (such as a closed box or given a user choice that this is not the box of the corrected type: With no partition or bipartitioned), the machine does not stop working but simply discards the box and restart the process keeping in memory the previous choice. We may get stuck in our model only in the case when the pieces are finished and the machine is not recharged, but we can assume that if there are no more pieces, it is correct that the process stops and restarts when new pieces are inserted by another machine; we can conclude that our system is robust.

Some of the properties that were verified in the UPPAAL tool on the previous TA are

1. A [] deadlock: NOT SATISFIED
   This property is not satisfied; in fact in the system, we never have deadlocks.

2. A[]Process.start imply key==1: SATISFIED
   The physical system can be used only if the key is inserted, so only a person with the key can turn on the machine. If in the automaton the state start is reached, it means that the key was inserted. If at a certain moment someone removes the key, the machine continues working until it finishes the current process. Once it has finished, the screen shows and alert stating that in order to start, the key is needed.

3. A[]Process.bolts imply choice==0: SATISFIED
   The state bolts are reached only if the choice was 0, then only if the choice was bolts. This property ensures that once a user do a choice, so given a specific input (in this case bolts desired), the system will give always the correct output (the box will contain bolts).

4. A[] (Process.discarded imply (((choice==0 or choice==1) and (openBox==0 or box==2)) or (choice==2 and (openBox==0 or box==1)))): SATISFIED
   When the system reaches the discarded node, it means that the box was closed, or with respect to the choice, the type of the box (with no partitions or bipartitioned) was not correct. The property, in fact, is that if the choice is 0 or 1 (bolts or nuts), then we need the box of type 1 (with no partition), but if the box is of the other type (bipartitioned → box==2), then the box is discarded; if the choice was of both bolts and nuts (choice==2), then the type of box needed is the box bipartitioned (box==2), but if there is a box with no partition (box==1), then the box is discarded. Whatever the choice (0,

1 or 2), if a box arrives that is closed (openBox==0), then it is discarded.

5. A[](Process.singleBox0 or Process.singleBox1) imply (open-Box==1 and box==1): SATISFIED

    If we are in the singleBox0 node or in the singleBox1 node, it means that the choice was only bolts or only nuts, respectively, and we reach these states only if the box is of the correct type. In this case, we need the box with no partition, and also the box needs to be open because if the box is closed, then it is discarded, and there is a "restart" where the choice made by the user remains in memory.

6. A[](Process.laststep and choice==0) imply (counterBolts == numberBolts): SATISFIED

    If we are in the state last step and the choice was bolts, then the counterBolts (i.e., a counter used to count how many pieces are inserted in the box) should be equal to the desired number of bolts selected before by the user (numberBolts). The same happens when the choice is nuts, then the number of nuts selected by the user should be equal to the counterNuts that count how many nuts are inserted in the box:

    A[](Process.laststep and choice==1) imply (counterNuts == numberNuts): SATISFIED

7. A[](Process.laststep and choice==2) imply (counterNuts == numberNuts and counterBolts == numberBolts and number-Bolts == numberNuts): SATISFIED

    If the choice was of both nuts and bolts, once we arrive in the state last step the number of nuts desired by the user should be equal to the counterNuts, and the same for the desired number of bolts should be equal to the pieces of bolts inside the box (counterBolts). We can also demonstrate that as the number of bolts selected from the user is the same of the number of nuts, then in the box at the end, we will have the same number of pieces of bolts and nuts.

2.4.1.1 Temporal Properties One of the advantages of converting the PLC program into a TA-based model is that it will be able to verify the PLC program with respect to temporal properties. In order to exploit this quality, here we checked our model with these following temporal properties, and the results are given below.

A <> Process.boxclosed: NOT SATISFIED

It denotes that eventually all boxes will be closed. But, in case of some faults in the filling processes of nuts and bolts, some boxes may not be closed. So, UPPAAL correctly identifies this property as false.

Similarly A <>! (Process.boxclosed): SATISFIED denotes the negation of the above property and it's also satisfied by UPPAAL.

E <> Process.boxclosed: SATISFIED

This property denotes that there exists a possibility that the boxes will be closed and this property will be satisfied by UPPAAL.

2.5 Experimental Results

In order to evaluate the performance of our proposed verification system, we tested the transformation system on various PLC codes, ranging from simple If-Else loops to the complex Nuts Bolts problem.

Table 2.1 gives the details of the experimental environment and Table 2.2 describes some preliminary results, where the transformation time refers to the total time to generate the .xta file from a PLC code, and verification time denotes the time taken by the UPPAAL verifier to execute one single verification property.

Notice that the transformation time is linear with respect to the size of the tested programs, while the verification time highly depends on the number of states of the generated automaton, possibly suffering from the state explosion problem. This issue can be faced either by applying trace partitioning techniques to the original PLC code or by splitting the model into non-interfering submodels and then by integrating the verification results.

Table 2.1 Experimental Setup

TOOL	VERSION	PURPOSE
Eclipse IDE – Xtext	2020-03 (4.15.0)	Generate domain-specific language (DSL)
Acceleo	2020-03 (4.15.0)	Model to text generator
Dev-C++	5.11	Process the text file generated by Acceleo and generate the .xta file
UPPAAL	4.1.22	Modeling and verification

Table 2.2 Experimental Results

CODE	NO. OF LOOPS	NO. OF LINES	TRANSFORMATION TIME (SEC)	VERIFICATION TIME (SEC)
Simple If-Else	1	19	5.88	0.002
Simple While	1	21	4.226	0.002
While+If-Else	2	26	4.916	0.003
Nested If	5	20	6.283	0.002
Mutual Exclusion	2	20	6.78	0.002
Pizza in a oven	4	60	6.317	0.003
Nuts & Bolts	16	121	8.354	0.006
2 D interpolator	2	30	5.81	0.002
Square,oot	1	21	4.657	0.002
Sorting	4	48	5.797	0.003

As mentioned before, we made use of PLCVerif as a back-to-back testing workbench to check our results, though the frequent occurrence of internal errors in PLCVerif prevents us to perform a systematic comparison of the two systems.

2.6 Conclusion

The framework for robustness analysis discussed in this chapter mainly consists in transforming a PLC program written in the SCL into a DSL with Xtext, then generating the .xta file with the help of Acceleo in Eclipse and yielding a TA that soundly corresponds to the initial program. Finally, robustness is checked by using UPPAAL as a model checker.

As the model checking suffers with the state explosion problem, for industrial software which are simple enough to be represented by a limited number of states, this approach is effective, whereas for complex systems either other techniques should be applied or a model splitting approach can be followed as we did in our case study, as a viable solution when no subtle interleaving occurs between submodels.

Acknowledgments

The work is partially supported by the project "Additive Manufacturing Industry 4.0 as Innovation Driver (ADMIN 4D)".

References

1. A. K. Mandal, A. Cortesi, A. Sarkar, and N. Chaki, "Things as a service: Service model for IoT". Proc. IEEE International Conference on Industrial Informatics (INDIN), 2019-July, art. no. 8972241, pp. 1364–1369, 2019.
2. W. C. Yew, "PLC Device Security – Tailoring needs", SANS Institute Information Security Reading Room, February 15, 2017.
3. R. Johnson, "Survey of SCADA security challenges and potential attack vectors", in Proceedings of International Conference for Internet Technology and Secured Transactions (ICITST), London, UK: IEEE, 2010.
4. H. Wardak, S. Zhioua, and A. Almulhem, "PLC access control: a security analysis," 2016 World Congress on Industrial Control Systems Security (WCICSS), London, UK, pp. 1–6, 2016. doi:10.1109/WCICSS.2016.7882935
5. Y. Wang, J. Liu, C. Yang, L. Zhou, S. Li, and Z. Xu, "Access control attacks on PLC vulnerabilities," Journal of Computer and Communications, vol. 6, pp. 311–325, 2018.
6. Z. Basnight, J. Butts, J. L. Jr., and T. Dube, "Firmware modification attacks on programmable logic controllers," International Journal of Critical Infrastructure Protection, vol. 6, no. 2, pp. 76–84, 2013.
7. L. Garcia and S. A. Zonouz, "Hey, My Malware Knows Physics! Attacking PLCs with Physical Model Aware Rootkit," in Proceedings of the 2017 Network and Distributed System Security Symposium (NDSS '17), 2017.
8. A. Abbasi and M. Hashemi, "Ghost in the PLC: Designing an Undetectable Programmable Logic Controller Rootkit via Pin Control Attack," in Black Hat Europe '16, pp. 1–35, November 2016.
9. L. Cojocar, K. Razavi, and H. Bos, "Off-the-Shelf Embedded Devices as Platforms for Security Research," in Proceedings of the 10th European Workshop on Systems Security (EuroSec'17), pp. 1:1–1:6, April 2017.
10. S. Yang, L. C. Cheng, and M. C. Chuah, "Detecting payload attacks on programmable logic controllers (PLCs)," IEEE Conference on Communications and Network Security (CNS), pp. 1–9, 2018. doi:10.1109/cns.2018.8433146
11. J. O. Malchow, D. Marzin, J. Klick, R. Kovacs, and V. Roth, "PLC Guard: A Practical Defense against Attacks on Cyber-Physical Systems," in 2015 IEEE Conference on Communications and Network Security (CNS), September 2015, pp. 326–334.
12. H. Janicke, A. Nicholson, S. Webber, and A. Cau, "Runtime-monitoring for industrial control Systems," Electronics, vol. 4, no. 4, pp. 995–1017, December 2015.
13. S. E. McLaughlin, S. A. Zonouz, D. J. Pohly, and P. D. McDaniel, "A Trusted Safety Verifier for Process Controller Code," in Proceedings of the 2014 Network and Distributed System Security Symposium (NDSS '14), 2014.

14. S. Zonouz, J. Rrushi, and S. McLaughlin, "Detecting industrial control malware using automated PLC code analytics," IEEE Security Privacy, vol. 12, no. 6, pp. 40–47, November 2014.

15. P. Ferrara, A. K. Mandal, A. Cortesi, and F. Spoto, "Static analysis for discovering IoT vulnerabilities," International Journal on Software Tools for Technology Transfer, vol. 23, pp. 71–88, 2021.

16. A. Mandal, P. Ferrara, Y. Khlyebnikov, A. Cortesi, and F. Spoto, "Cross-program taint analysis for IoT systems". Proceedings of the ACM Symposium on Applied Computing, pp. 1944–1952, 2020.

17. J.-C. Fernandez, L. Mounier, and C. Pachon, "A model-based approach for robustness testing". In: Khendek F. and Dssouli R. (eds), Testing of Communicating Systems. TestCom 2005. Lecture Notes in Computer Science, vol. 3502. Berlin, Heidelber: Springer, p. 333–348, 2005.

18. G. Behrmann, A. David, and K. G. Larsen, "A tutorial on UPPAAL," In Formal Methods for the Design of Real-Time Systems, Springer, pp. 200–236, 2004.

19. D. Soliman, K. Thramboulidis, and G. Frey, "Transformation of function block diagrams to UPPAAL timed automata," Annual Reviews in Control, vol. 36, pp. 338–345, 2012.

20. K. Thramboulidis, D. Soliman, and G. Frey, "Towards an automated verification process for industrial safety applications," In IEEE 7th International Conference on Automation Science and Engineering (IEEE CASE 2011). August 24–27, Trieste, Italy.

21. CERN. PLCVerif verification tool (2020). https://readthedocs.web.cern.ch/display/ICKB/PLCverif/

22. G. Canet, S. Couffin, J. Lesage, A. Petit, and P. Schnoebelen, "Towards the automatic verification of PLC programs written in Instruction List," SMC 2000 conference proceedings. 2000 IEEE international conference on systems, man and cybernetics. 'Cybernetics evolving to systems, humans, organizations, and their complex interactions' (cat. no.0), Nashville, TN, vol.4., pp. 2449–2454, 2000, doi:10.1109/ICSMC.2000.884359

23. O. Rossi, O. de Smet, S. Lamp'eri`ere-Couffin, J.-J. Lesage, H. Papini, and H. Guennec, Formal verification: a tool to improve the safety of control systems. In 4th Symposium on Fault Detection, Supervision and Safety for Technical Processes (IFAC Safeprocess 2000), Budapest, Hungary, 2000.

24. Siemens, SIMATIC Programming with STEP7 – Manual, 2010, A5E02789666-01.

25. Siemens, SIMATIC Structured Control Language (SCL) for S7-300/S7-400 Programming Manual, 6ES7811-1CA02-8BA0.

26. White paper, "PLC programming in the age of IoT."

27. P. Ferrara, A. Cortesi, and F. Spoto, "From CIL to Java bytecode: semantics-based translation for static analysis leveraging," Science of Computer Programming, 102392, 2020. doi:10.1016/j.scico.2020.102392

28. K. Bjorkman, J. Frits, J. Valkonen, J. Lahtinen, K. Heljanko, I. Niemelä, and J. Hamalainen, "Verification of safety logic designs by model checking," Proceedings of the Sixth American Nuclear Society International Topical Meeting on Nuclear Plant Instrumentation, Control, and Human-Machine Interface Technologies NPICHMIT 2009. American Nuclear Society ANS, 2009.

Appendix A: Bolts and Nuts SCL Code

```
/* b o l t s and nuts */
FUNCTION TEST: INT
VAR_INPUT
key : INT;
choice : INT;
input : INT;
input 1 : INT;
input 2 : INT;
input 3 : INT;
input 4 : INT;
box : INT;
openBox : INT;
numberBolts : INT;
numberNuts : INT;
END_VAR
VAR_OUTPUT
counterBolts : INT;
counterNuts : INT;
close : BOOL;
position Push : BOOL;
END_VAR
VAR
mainConveyor : BOOL;
conveyorB : BOOL;
conveyorN : BOOL;
pieces B : INT;
pieces N : INT;
recharge B : BOOL;
recharge N : BOOL;
position : BOOL;
push : BOOL;
discard : BOOL;
i : INT;
j : INT;
k : INT;
END_VAR
```

```
BEGIN
WHILE true DO
IF    key==0    THEN
     mainConveyor:= false;
ELSEIF key==1 THEN
     mainConveyor:= true;
     choice : = input;
               IF    choice==0 THEN
                  box:= input 1;
                  openBox:= input 2;
                  IF    box==2    OR openBox==0 THEN
                        discard : = true;
                        i : = 0;
                  ELSEIF   box==1  AND    openBox==1 THEN
                      numberBolts : = input 3;
                      mainConveyor:=     false;
                      IF    pieces B==0 THEN
                           recharge B : = true;
                             END_IF;
                             WHILE    pieces B==1 AND i
                             <numberBolts DO
                                   conveyorB:= true;
                                    counterBolts : =
                                    counterBolts + 1;
                                      i : = i + 1;
                             END_WHILE;
                             conveyorB:= false;
                             mainConveyor:= true;
                     END_IF;
               ELSEIF  choice==1 THEN
                    box:= input 1;
                    openBox:= input 2;
                    IF    box==2 OR openBox==0 THEN
                          discard : = true;
                          j : = 0;
                    ELSEIF   box==1 AND openBox==1 THEN
                             numberNuts:= input 4;
                             mainConveyor:= false;
                             IF   pieces N==0 THEN
                                 recharge N : = true;
                             END_IF;
                             WHILE    pieces N==1 AND j
                              <numberNuts DO
                                   conveyorN : = true;
```

```
                        counter Nuts : =
                        counter Nuts+ 1;
                             j:=j+ 1;
                END_WHILE;
                conveyorN : = false;
                mainConveyor:= true;
            END_IF;
      ELSEIF choice==2 THEN
          box:= input 1;
          openBox:= input 2;
          IF   box==1 OR  openBox==0 THEN
                discard : = true;
                k : = 0;
        ELSEIF  box==1 AND openBox==1 THEN
                numberBolts : = input 3;
                numberNuts:= numberBolts;
                mainConveyor:= false;
                IF   pieces N==0 THEN
              recharge N : = true;
                END_IF;
                WHILE   pieces N==1 AND
                k<numberNuts DO
                        conveyorN : = true;
                        counter Nuts : =
                        counter Nuts+ 1;
                        k:=k+ 1;
                END_WHILE;
                conveyorN : = false;
                mainConveyor:= true;
                        k : = 0;
                END_IF;
                mainConveyor:= false;
                IF   pieces B==0 THEN
                        recharge B : = true;
                WHILE pieces B==1 AND
                k<numberBolts DO
                   conveyorB:= true;
                        counterBolts : =
                        counterBolts+ 1;
                        k:=k+ 1;
                END_WHILE;
                        conveyorB:= false;
                        mainConveyor:= true;
      END_IF;
```

```
        END_IF;
        IF position==true    THEN
                    mainConveyor:= false;
                    close : = true;
          END_IF;
          close : = false;
          mainConveyor:= true;
          IF    position Push==true THEN
              push:= true;
              counter Nuts : = 0;
              counterBolts : = 0;
          END_IF;
END_IF;
END_WHILE;
END_FUNCTION
```

Appendix B: Timed Automata of the Nuts and Bolts System

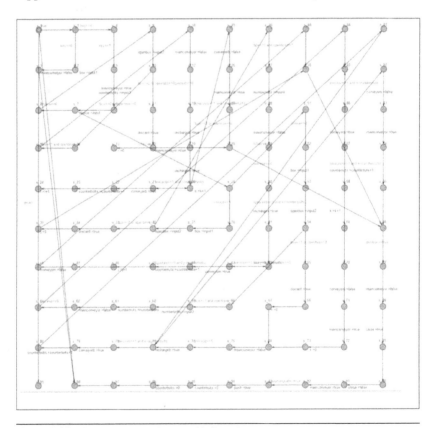

Figure 2.10   Timed automata of nuts and bolts system.

3

MACHINE ETHICS ASPECTS IN THE INTERNET OF THINGS

EWA ŁUKASIK

Poznań University of Technology, Poznań, Poland

Contents

3.1 Introduction

The term Machine Ethics (ME) still seems overstated for engineers and even threatening for ordinary people. In the best cases, it is associated with philosophy, if not with science fiction novels. The term was born on the junction of Artificial Intelligence (AI) and philosophy [2–4]. It became well established in the multidisciplinary discourse in such domains as AI, robotics, computing, philosophy and sociology [5, 6–10]. Anderson [2] has presented its definition: "Machine Ethics is concerned with the consequences of the behavior of machines towards human users and other machines." ME provides models and implementation trials of autonomous moral artificial agents for various

DOI: 10.1201/9781003149507-3

applications, e.g., an ethically responsive robot assisting people or AI advisors with ethical issues in medicine. Most of the AI threats are linked with robots taking over humans and lethal autonomous weapons. However, the true danger may come unnoticeably: misaligned AI may control the humanity disembodied – through the Internet [39] or, more precisely, through the Internet of Things (IoT). A dense mesh of Wireless Sensor Networks continually feeds the Internet with raw or processed/interpreted data that are further processed by powerful AI algorithms at the edge or in a cloud. Such a scenario will be expected soon. Nonetheless, in this context (IoT), the ME problems appear relatively rare, though social, ethical and legal problems have been noticed and addressed in several journals and conferences, e.g. [1, 23]. Currently, at this stage of development, the IoT domain faces enormous problems related to cybersecurity and privacy, so the moral performance of intelligent agents interconnected by the global network of the IoT infrastructure seems to be too far-reaching. But the question asked by Berman and Cerf [7] sounds "How do we promote the ethical issues within the IoT technologies? Whose ethics should be applied?"

This chapter aims to present some ethical issues related to the IoT as an extension to the problem of its security and privacy. It is a broad subject, and covering most of its aspects, discussions, pro and con arguments, even in the IoT's narrowed context, is far beyond this chapter's limits. Interested readers can refer to the latest publications on this topic [49–55, 60, 61]. Here, we set up one of the voices promoting the need for discussion, research and education on ethics in the domain of the IoT. We consider IoT as the Internet of interconnected intelligent agents that may cause problems related to ME in the future generation computing systems. We will also show the need to build the awareness of ethical problems among the students of IoT and practitioners. Some issues from this chapter were presented during the conference Machine Ethics and Machine Law (MEML'2016) in Cracow, Poland [22, 29].

The paper is structured as follows: Section 3.2 will present core concepts related to ME, the IoT and artificial agents necessary for further discussion. Section 3.3 will review the diversity of ethical systems being developed within the philosophy domain and some trials to incorporate them into ME models. Section 3.4 will explain the rationale for discussing ME issues from the IoT perspective. Section 3.5 will present international initiatives developing and popularizing ME problems worldwide. Section 3.6 concludes the chapter.

3.2 Core Concepts

3.2.1 Machine Ethics

Machine Ethics (ME) was established on the ground of Artificial Intelligence (AI), and its foundations have been laid in 60s and popularized by Anderson, who defined it as being concerned "with the consequences of behavior of machines towards human users and other machines" [2]. The term "machine" is usually understood as a combination of software and hardware. A machine's "behavior" is rather related to intelligent machines that are more or less autonomous. Anderson further writes:

> an ethical dimension in machines could be used to alert humans who rely on machines before they do something that is ethically questionable, averting harm that might have been caused otherwise. Also, machine-machine relationships could benefit from this ethical dimension, providing a basis for resolving resource conflict or predicting behavior of other machines. Working in the area of machine ethics could have the additional benefit of forcing us to sharpen our thinking in ethics and enable us to discover problems with current ethical theories. This may lead to "improved ethical theories.

Since then, these words remain relevant to this day. Many research questions have been asked about the ME, how feasible it is to design an artificial agent possessing ethical properties. The ME became an emerging field that seeks to implement moral decision-making faculties in computers and robots. More emphasis in a practical ME was on moral productivity, not receptivity, in the sense that a moral agent has its own ethical demands and rights, alongside with humans [40].

3.2.2 From the Internet of Things to Agents of Things

Among many quoted definitions of the IoT, one is often missing, i.e., from the Recommendation ITU-T T.2060, that was in 2016 renumbered as

ITU-T y.4000 (without further modification and without being repub-
lished) [25] that clearly states that IoT is "a global infrastructure for
the information society, enabling advanced services by interconnecting
physical and virtual things based on existing and evolving interoperable
information and communication technologies." It is interesting how the
Recommendation defines a thing: "A physical thing may be represented
in the information world via one or more virtual things (mapping), but
a virtual thing can also exist without any associated physical thing." It
means that a piece of software may be treated as a thing. The requirement
sets some obligations on the IoT system, including the interoperability
among heterogeneous and distributed systems, autonomic networking
(self-management, self-configuring, self-healing, self-protecting) and
autonomic services provisioning.

The International Organization for Standardization/ International
Electrotechnical Commission (ISO/IEC) definition of the IoT is
somehow similar [24]: "An infrastructure of interconnected objects,
people, systems and information resources together with intelligent
services to allow them to process information of the physical and the
virtual world and react."

The convergence of the natural environment with technology will
lead to the creation of hybrid ecologies. The responsibility for both
humans and autonomous machines (robots, autonomous vehicles,
etc.) will be highly interdependent. Operations will rely on many data,
decisions and services of distant, often unknown sources, and may
cause possible unethical decisions.

On the other hand, let us return to AI, which is distinguished
through agents' notion – entities that perceive and act [35, 36].
Intelligent agents continuously perform three functions:

- *Perception* of dynamic conditions in the environment
- *Action* to affect conditions in the environment
- *Reasoning* to interpret perceptions, solve problems, draw infer-
  ences and determine actions [47], making intermediate decisions that other agents will rely on and use for their decisions.

Agents may have various degrees of perceived intelligence and may
be close to the hierarchical structures performing complicated tasks.
Taking into account the above characteristics of artificial agents and
the definition of things that may be virtual, i.e., in the form of pieces

of software, it seems natural to put the sign of equality between them and accept the notion Agents of Things (AoT) as was introduced by Mzahm [32]. In this way, the IoT gains reasoning and intelligent features. Fortino has adopted this idea as Agent-oriented IoT Systems [15]. Thus, we can talk about the IoT/AoT system of interconnected AI agents that may mutually impact each other's behavior without the human control.

3.3 Ethical Systems for AI

Despite the globalization and democratization of the contemporary world, moral systems still vary across cultures and societal levels. Ethics have a complex nature. Thus, the first dilemma the specialists try to solve is constructing a universal moral system for AI. Dignum [10] observed that

> methodologies are needed to elicit the values held by designers and stakeholders, design methods and tools to elicit and represent human values, translate these values into technical requirements and deal with moral overload when numerous values are to be incorporated ... to demonstrate that design solutions realize the values wished for.

AI systems are proposed to be grounded on Accountability, Responsibility and Transparency (ART) principles, extending classic principles of Autonomy, Interactivity and Adaptability [14, 36]:

- *Accountability* for decision must be derivable from the algorithm including moral and societal values.
- *Responsibility* – if AI causes action, it must be clear chain of responsibility of designers.
- *Transparency* – for explaining actions.

To fulfill these principles, the system should be based on ethical considerations, and moral consequences should be taken into account. This should happen early in an agent's lifetime, already at the design stage of the project, when design decisions are formulated explicitly. Value Sensitive Design proposed by Friedman in 1996 [16] was later followed by others, especially by Van den Hoven [41] as Design for Values. The method takes moral values into account on the system design stage and then iteratively uses them on other system development life stages.

The moral values vary with the ethical theories that might be incorporated to the intelligent agent or the system. They span from *human-centric*, focusing on the subject (creator and user) who knows the laws governing technical entities and brings them to the role of tools, to *posthumanistic*, granting full morality to new non-human entities [30], e.g., *human-robot blends* [22] or *more-than-human* ones [40].

Dignum [10] recalls three categories of normative ethical theories (indicating which actions are good and bad and how to value things by a set of norms) considering them the most useful for AI:

- *Consequentialism* – an action is morally right if it results in good consequence (results matter); however, there must be a body that has the means to judge its consequences.
- *Deontology* – judges the morality of actions based on rules – an action is morally right if it follows a moral rule or principle (e.g. a person can never be used as a means).
- *Virtue Ethics* concentrates more on a person and his/her motifs than on the consequences of their actions.

Torrence [40] discusses four other categories that are possible for ME: *Anthropocentrism, Infocentrism, Biocentrism* and *Ecocentrism*. Despite deep oppositions between them, three opponents of anthropocentrism tend to extend merely beyond human ethical values. *Anthropocentrism* would see ME as a domain of intelligent systems engineering problems, not developing machines as ethical agents in their own right. *Infocentrism* is a hope that technology will deploy autonomous artificial agents more responsible and humanity-respecting [40]. *Biocentrism* extends the boundary of moral standing as far as it is possible: all living beings have moral standing and deserve moral consideration. *Ecocentrism* denotes a nature-centered, as opposed to human-centered (i.e., anthropocentric), system of values.

Rarely, *personalism* is recalled in this context, despite it emphasizes the significance, uniqueness and inviolability of the person, as well as the person's essentially relational or social dimension [48]. However, strong voices calling for respect for traditional and cultural values and not searching for new ones are not rare. Bryson, in many other writings and speeches, stands firmly in the position that we, people, should not lose our superiority over the AI, and all ethical and legal systems should not change this situation "AI works best as a sort of mental prosthetic to our own needs and desires." [8]

Implementing different theories will cause different algorithmic and computational problems, including the algorithms' computational complexity [10], resulting in the ME's economic aspect. Thus, e.g., in *Moral Machines*, Wallach and Collin [46] claim that it doesn't matter whether artificial systems are genuine moral agents, but the results of their operations matter. They state that

> The engineering objective remains the same: humans need advanced (ro)bots to act as much like moral agents as possible. All things considered, advanced automated systems that use moral criteria to rank different courses of action are preferable to ones that pay no attention to moral issues.

3.4 Ethical Issues Related to the IoT

3.4.1 Current Perception of the IoT

Technology, business and even human consciousness all rely on IoT [17]. The research is directed toward approaches that allow things to become smarter, more reliable and more autonomous, simply – more intelligent [27]. New architectures are proposed permitting things to learn from others' experiences, capture social behavior and preserve privacy. Smart devices provide a basis for smart homes, smart cities, smart cars, etc. The constantly evolving IoT requires continual software adaptation, moving toward mobile agents' applications [15, 32]. Autonomic things will allow systems to self-manage the complexity, to control the dynamicity of growth and the IoT distribution [28]. They will evolve to create the knowledge out of data and rules discovered during the operation.

The main concern of the IoT ecosystem architects is the privacy protection support, cybersecurity, data in motion and data at rest defenses [44]. Also, the needs for equal access are addressed, especially in high quality and highly secure.

As the infrastructure and services of IoT grow, the human opinion is driven toward the benefits that the technology brings, e.g., utility, well-being, sustainability, health, safety and security. However, it is still unclear how the IoT affects global trends across all spheres of the human existence. Being distributed in various locations, things activate big data difficult to be efficiently and automatically managed, analyzed and understood. Equipped with intelligent software agents, they will make intermediate decisions that other agents will rely on and use for their decisions. In this way, IoT, with all its sensors, cameras and microphones, is becoming a huge AI system.

3.4.2 Morally Relevant Aspects of the IoT

The IoT-constrained features impose considerable difficulties in modeling the behavior of ethical agents. Whether they are rule- or data-driven – they can hardly predict their behavior in a complicated ecosystem. Howard and Muntean [20] propose a model for an artificial autonomous moral agent (AAMA), which is minimal in its ethical assumptions. Starting from a set of moral data, AAMA can learn and develop a form of moral competency. As a drawback, the authors see the dependency on the data, their reliability, or how they were collected. Moral agents, according to Wallach and Collin [46], may stand at the third level of ethical entities, i.e., over operational tools (e.g., searching machines) and functional assistants (sensitive to ethical features of their environment).

Some clues for approaching the problem of ME in an IoT environment can be taken from the seminal paper of Floridi and Sanders [14], where the Method of Abstraction for analyzing the level of abstraction (LoA) is proposed at which an agent is considered to act. The LoA is determined by how one chooses to describe, analyze and discuss a system and its context. The moral agenthood depends on an LoA. This approach was criticized by Grodzinsky et al. [18]. The radical view was also presented by Hew [19], who claimed that "with foreseeable technologies, an artificial agent will carry zero responsibility for its behavior, and humans will retain full responsibility," and Deng [9] concluded "We need some serious progress to figure out what's relevant for AI to reason successfully in ethical situations." Computer scientists that were trying to respond to this question used to rely mainly on logic rules. This approach may work in static circumstances, but taking decisions in a dynamically changing ecosystem is much more complicated and less predictable [9]. Moral arguments in favor of the IoT are also accompanied by those raising its dangers and possible preventive measures. Authors, e.g., Popescul and Georgescu [34], Ebersold and Glass [11], often recall Wachtel Report of EC meeting [45] and van den Hoven [42, 43], where 11 defining features of IoT were characterized causing the ethical problems, some of them being recalled below:

- Ambiguous criteria of identity and system boundaries because of an easy transformation of natural objects, artefacts, and human beings,
- Electronic identity of objects with various levels of importance, crucial for IoT, but difficult to be managed; even if not maliciously used, they may be simply wrongly managed or erroneous.
- Unprecedented degree of connectivity between objects and humans in networks (connectivity)
- Spontaneous and unexpected (for users and designers) interference of interconnected objects driven by autonomous agents
- Objects with embedded intelligence will make humans feel cognitively and physically handicapped; some will not accept the embodiment of extended mind.

There are concerns about the IoT's distributed control and governance that will face unpredictable problems and uncertainty. Neither a human nor an autonomous machine will have the relevant knowledge to make the right/ethical decisions.

Mittelstadt [31] has reviewed over 128 sources (out of 1108 nonunique ones), the papers related to ethics of the Health-related Internet of Things (H-IoT), and identified the following ethical topics (some of them going beyond machine-only ethics):

- Personal and information privacy,
- Obtrusiveness (effects that perceived as undesirable),
- Lack of autonomy and data sharing,
- Social isolation,
- Consent and the uncertain value of H-IoT data, their ownership and access,
- Decontextualization of health and well-being,
- Risks of nonprofessional care

Van den Hoven group [42] expects the remedial response for those constraints in Value Sensitive Design [16], i.e., values built into systems and responsible design of sociotechnical systems. Engineers are choice architects who design for X, where X is, e.g., privacy, inclusion, sustainability, democracy, safety, transparency, accountability or human capabilities. At this stage, the conflicting social values may be considered in a way warranting a win–win result. Values are hierarchically structured and then translated into requirements [10].

3.5 Machine Ethics Promoting Initiatives

M. Anderson and S. L. Anderson have been the introducers and advocates of Machine Ethics, promoting the idea of giving machines' ethical principles and procedures to resolve the ethical dilemmas [2–5]. They cochaired the AAAI Fall 2005 Symposium on Machine Ethics, coedited an IEEE Intelligent Systems' special issue on ME [3], coauthored an invited article on the topic for Artificial Intelligence Magazine [4] and, in 2011, edited a fundamental book on ME containing 31 chapters written by distinguished authors in the field [5].

With the enormously fast progress of AI toward the so-called Artificial General Intelligence (AGI or strong AI – the hypothetical ability of an intelligent agent to understand or learn any intellectual task that a human being can), the leading AI researchers started to warn the scientific community about potential risks the technology may bring and to raise the concern about risks posed by developing AI. The researchers who met during The Future of AI: Opportunities and Challenges conference in Puerto Rico in 2015 [1] tried to predict how and when it will be possible to create human-level AI in the recent AI explosive development. They also defined research priorities for robust and beneficial AI (including ME) [37] and published an Open Letter with the recommendation that expanded research aimed at ensuring that increasingly capable AI systems are robust and beneficial. Up to date, the Letter has been signed by 8000 people, with the father of AI – Stuart Russel, as the first name in the list. This Open Letter has triggered the increase in conferences and seminars devoted to the problems of Machine Ethics and Machine Law, e.g., AAAI Spring Symposium on Ethical and Moral Considerations in Nonhuman Agents in Palo Alto, the IEEE Summit devoted to Artificial Intelligence and Ethics in Brussels, (http://ieee-summit.org/programme/ [21]), International Conference Machine Ethics and Machine Law in Kraków, Poland [23] and Zagreb Applied Ethics Conference.

There are also official documents concerning ME. Recently European Parliament has issued a study on European Civil Law Rules in Robotics, the resolution with recommendations to the European Commission [13, 26], which was somehow critically discussed by the group member working on the Code of Ethics for AI [12]. IEEE has launched a global initiative IEEE Ethics in Action "To ensure every stakeholder involved in the design and development of autonomous and intelligent systems is educated, trained, and empowered to prioritize ethical considerations so that these technologies are advanced for the benefit of humanity" and issued a document "Ethically Aligned Design" presenting a vision for prioritizing "Human Well-being with Autonomous and Intelligent Systems" [56]. In 2017, during the Asilomar Conference, the Asilomar AI Principles were proclaimed [57], and in the same year, Barcelona Declaration for the Proper Development and Usage of Artificial Intelligence in Europe [58] and Top 10 Principles for Ethical Artificial Intelligence [59] were issued.

In the USA, the Executive Office of the President issued a document in December 2016: Artificial Intelligence, Automation and the Economy, preceded by another document, the Future of Artificial Intelligence prepared by the National Science and Technology Council [33], raising many issues, including fairness, safety and governance. Growing number of journal articles is devoted to ME as well as journals' special issues (e.g., Proceedings of the IEEE [60]) and conferences. To summarize them, the review papers are published to recapitulate the research in ME [51, 52, 54, 55, 61]. To involve students in the discussion on AI and Ethics, the ACM organized the ACM SIGAI Student Essay Contest on the Responsible Use of Artificial Intelligence (AI) Technologies [38] that brought several interesting opinions of young people.

All the abovementioned initiatives brought practical outcomes. Universities offer short programs in ethical design [50] and create tools and application modules to include ethics in design [52, 53]. As may be expected, their application in the IoT is also present [49].

The author of this chapter often discusses the subject presented in the article with students of IoT in his mother institute which meets the students' interests. The practical results will be the subject of a forthcoming paper.

3.6 Conclusions

In this chapter, we have presented some issues related to ME in the dynamically evolving world, where AI is becoming more and more influential within the dense mesh of the IoT. Because of its complexity, dependability, unpredictability, and dynamics, IoT will become hard to manage as a whole by humans and machines operated by humans. Ensuring decision-making or delegating ethical responsibility to any other entity than human is regarded as unacceptable. On the other hand, the Internet with AI algorithms standing behind will be a huge distributed superintelligence with interdependencies difficult to follow and difficult to be closed in frames of ethical and legal norms. But ethical issues in the context of intelligent machines and things have to be studied and popularized among students and IT practitioners. Constant discussions and research efforts should be made to keep people informed. Promoting awareness of ethical risks from the Internet of AI Things among researchers, engineers, students and ordinary people is imperative. It may also bring people unexpected benefits of closer adhesion to valid ethical norms.

References

1. AI Safety conference: The Future of AI: Opportunities and Challenges, Puerto Rico (2015), https://futureoflife.org/2015/10/12/ai-safety-conference-in-puerto-rico/ (accessed 27.02.2021)
2. M. Anderson, S.L. Anderson, C. Armen, Towards Machine Ethics, Proc. of the AOTP'04 (2004).
3. M. Anderson, S.L. Anderson, eds., Special Issue on Machine Ethics, IEEE Intelligent Systems 21(4), (2006).
4. M. Anderson, S.L. Anderson, Machine Ethics: Creating an Ethical Intelligent Agent, AI Magazine 28(4), (2007), 15–26.
5. M. Anderson, S.L. Anderson, eds., Machine Ethics: Cambridge University Press, (2011).
6. K. Ashton, That "Internet of Things" Thing, RFiD Journal (2009, June). http://www.rfidjournal.com/articles/view?4986 (accessed 27.07.2017)
7. F. Berman, V.G. Cerf, Social and Ethical Behavior in the Internet of Things, Communications of the ACM 60(2), (2017), 6–7.

8. J.J. Bryson, Patiency Is Not a Virtue: AI and the Design of Ethical Systems. Proceedings of the AAAI Spring Symposium on Ethical and Moral Considerations in Nonhuman Agents, Palo Alto, CA: AAAI Press, (2016), 202–207. https://www.aaai.org/ocs/index.php/SSS/SSS16/paper/view/12686/11951 (accessed 27.07.2017)

9. B. Deng, Machine Ethics: The Robot's Dilemma, Nature 523(7558), (2015), 24–26.

10. V. Dignum, Responsible Autonomy (2017), arXiv:1706.02513v1.

11. K. Ebersold, R. Glass, The Internet of Things: A Cause for Ethical Concern, Issues in Information Systems 17(IV), (2016), 145–151.

12. Ethics for Artificial Intelligence, https://www.cs.ox.ac.uk/efai/ (accessed 12.03.2021)

13. European Parliament, European Civil Law Rules in Robotics (2016) http://www.europarl.europa.eu/RegData/etudes/STUD/2016/571379/IPOL_STU(2016)571379_EN.pdf (accessed 12.03.2021)

14. L. Floridi, J.W. Sander, On the Morality of Artificial Agents, Minds and Machine 14, (2004), 349–379.

15. G. Fortino, W. Russo, C. Savaglio, Simulation of Agent-Oriented Internet of Things Systems. [In:] Proc. 17th Workshop "From Objects to Agents" (2016) 8–13.

16. B. Friedman, Value Sensitive Design, ACM Interactions 3(6), (1996), 17–23.

17. J. Greenough, How the Internet of Things Will Impact Consumers, Businesses, and Governments in 2016 and Beyond, Business Insider, July. (2016) www.businessinsider.com (accessed 28.07.2017)

18. F.S. Grodzinsky, K.W. Miller, M.J. Wolf, The Ethics of Designing Artificial Agents, Ethics and Information Technology 10(2–3), (2008), 115–121.

19. P.C. Hew, Artificial Moral Agents Are Infeasible with Foreseeable Technologies, Ethics and Information Technology 16(3), (2014), 197–206.

20. D. Howard, I. Muntean, A Minimalist Model of the Artificial Autonomous Moral Agent (AAMA). In AAAI Spring Symposium Series, (2016).

21. IEEE Summit: Artificial Intelligence and Ethics – Who Does the Thinking?, Brussels, (2016) http://ieee-summit.org/programme/ (accessed 12.03.2021)

22. B. Indurkhya, Is Morality the Last Frontier for Machines?, Proc. MEML'16, Kraków (2016).

23. B. Indurkhya, B. Brożek, G. Stojanov, eds., Machine Ethics and Machine Law, E-Proceedings, Kraków (2016).

24. ISO/IEC JTC 1, Internet of Things, Preliminary Report (2014).

25. ITU-T Recommendation Y.2060. Overview of the Internet of Things, (2012) https://www.itu.int/rec/T-REC-Y.2060-201206-I (accessed 27.02.2021)

26. M. Kritikos, Robotics as a New Object of EU's 'Ethical' Attention: Preliminary Considerations Concerning EP's Draft Report on Robotics, Proc. MEML'16, Kraków (2016).

27. D. Kyriazis, T. Varvarigou, Smart, Autonomous and Reliable Internet of Things, Procedia Computer Science, 21, (2013), 442–448.
28. T. Leppänen, J. Riekki, M. Liu, E. Harjula, T. Ojala, Mobile Agents-Based Smart Objects for the Internet of Things. In Fortino G. and Trunfio P. (eds.): Internet of Things Based on Smart Objects: Springer, (2014), 29–48.
29. E. Łukasik, Machine Ethics in the Internet of Things Environment (Extended Abstract), Proc. MEML'16, Kraków (2016).
30. J. Maliński, Meta-Ethical Requirements for Ethical Systems Concerning Inhuman Beings (in Polish), Abstract, Homo Informaticus 4.0, Poznan (2016).
31. B. Mittelstadt, Ethics of the Health-Related Internet of Things: A Narrative Review, Ethics and Information Technology, Open Access Article (2017), 1–19.
32. A.M. Mzahm, M.S. Ahmad, A.Y.C. Tang, Enhancing the Internet of Things (IoT) via the Concept of Agent of Things (AoT), Journal of Network and Innovative Computing, 2, (2014), 101–110.
33. National Science and Technology Council, Preparing for the Future of Artificial Intelligence, (2016) https://info.publicintelligence.net/WhiteHouse-ArtificialIntelligencePreparations.pdf (accessed 12.03.2021)
34. D. Popescul, M. Georgescu, Internet of Things – Some Ethical Issues. The USV Annals of Economics and Public Administration, 13(2), (2013), 208–214.
35. S. Russel, P. Norvig, Artificial Intelligence: A modern Approach (3rd Edition): Pearson Education, (2009).
36. S. Russel., Rationality and Intelligence: A Brief Update, (2016).
37. S. Russel, D. Dewey, M. Tegmark, Research Priorities for Robust and Beneficial Artificial Intelligence, AI Magazine, (Winter, 2015), 105–114.
38. Student Essay Contest on the Responsible Use of Artificial Intelligence (AI) Technologies, https://sigai.acm.org/aimatters/blog/2016/12/04/essaycontest/ (accessed 27.02.2021)
39. M. Tegmark, Benefits and Risks of Artificial Intelligence, Future of Life, https://futureoflife.org/
40. S. Torrence, Machine Ethics and the Idea of a More-Than-Human Moral World. In, Anderson M. and Anderson S. (eds.): Machine Ethics: Cambridge University Press, (2010).
41. J. Van den Hoven, Design for Values and Values for Design, Information Age+, Journal of the Australian Computer Society 7(2), (2005), 4–7.
42. J. Van Den, Ethics and The Internet of Things. European Commission. Delft University of Technology, (2012) http://ec.europa.eu/transparency/regexpert/index.cfm?do=groupDetail.groupDetailDoc&id=7607&no=4 (accessed 27.02.2021)
43. J. Van Den Hoven, J. Fact Sheet – Ethics Subgroup IoT – Ver. 4.0 (2014) http://digitalchampion.bg/uploads/agenda/en/filepath_85.pdf (accessed 27.02.2021)
44. Vormetric Global Insider Threat Report (2015), http://enterprise-encryption.vormetric.com/rs/vormetric/images/CW_GlobalReport_

2015_Insider_threat_Vormetric_Single_Pages_010915.pdf (accessed 27.07.20017)

45. T. Wachtel T. IoT Expert Group Final Meeting Report. European Commission, (14 November, 2012).

46. W. Wallach, A. Collin, Moral Machines: Oxford University Press, (2011).

47. B. Hayes-Roth, An Architecture for Adaptive Intelligent Systems, Artificial Intelligence 72, (1995), 329–365.

48. https://plato.stanford.edu/entries/personalism/ (accessed 10.03.2021)

49. G. Baldini, M. Botterman, R. Neisse, M. Tallacchini, Ethical Design in the Internet of Things, Science and Engineering Ethics 25, (2019), 1763–1770.

50. B. Taebi, W. E. Kastenberg, Teaching Engineering Ethics to PhD Students: A Berkeley–Delft Initiative, Science and Engineering Ethics 25, (2019), 1763–1770.

51. J.-A. Cervantes, S. López, L.-F. Rodríguez, S. Cervantes, F. Cervantes, F. Ramos, Artificial Moral Agents: A Survey of the Current Status, Science and Engineering Ethics 26,(2020), 501–532.

52. J. Morley, L. Floridi, L. Kinsey, A. Elhalal, From What to How: An Initial Review of Publicly Available AI Ethics Tools, Methods and Research to Translate Principles into Practices, Science and Engineering Ethics 26,(2020), 2141–2168.

53. L. Bezuidenhout, R. Quick, H. Shanahan, "Ethics When You Least Expect It": A Modular Approach to Short Course Data Ethics Instruction, Science and Engineering Ethics 26, (2020), 2189–2213.

54. V. Nallur, Landscape of Machine Implemented Ethics. Science and Engineering Ethics 26, (2020), 2381–2399.

55. W. A. Bauer, Expanding Nallur's Landscape of Machine Implemented Ethics, Science and Engineering Ethics 26, (2020), 2401–2410.

56. IEEE Ethics in Action https://ethicsinaction.ieee.org/ (accessed 10.03.2021)

57. Asilomar AI Principles, https://futureoflife.org/ai-principles/ (accessed 10.03.2021)

58. Barcelona Declaration for the Proper Development and Usage of Artificial Intelligence in Europe, https://www.iiia.csic.es/barcelonadeclaration/ (accessed 10.03.2021)

59. Top 10 Principles for Ethical Artificial Intelligence, http://www.thefutureworldofwork.org/media/35420/uni_ethical_ai.pdf (accessed 10.03.2021)

60. Machine Ethics: The Design and Governance of Ethical AI and Autonomous Systems, Proceedings of the IEEE (2019) vol.107, no 3.

61. S. Tolmeijer, M. Kneer, C. Sarasua, M. Christen, A. Bernstein, Implementations in Machine Ethics: A Survey, ACM Computing Surveys 53(6), Article 132, (December 2020).

4

AN INTRUSION DETECTION SYSTEM FOR WSN LAYER OF IoT

DEBDUTTA BARMAN ROY
AND RITUPARNA CHAKI

Contents

4.1 Introduction

Internet of Things (IoT) has clearly made it easy for the users to send or receive data whenever they wish, and by whichever device they want, such as smart TVs, smart watches, etc. As we have already discussed in Chapter 1, the data, on its path to the destination, passes through the four layers of Transmission Control Protocol/Internet Protocol (TCP/IP) communication suite, facing all the known attacks at each layer. There is a plethora of attacks in an IoT environment, targeted at the data being transmitted across the network (Figure 4.1). The data in transit may have to face attacks such as the man-in the-middle (MIM) attacks, sniffer attacks, denial-of-service (DoS), as well as the compromised-key attacks.

Out of these attacks, the DoS attack is an easy to implementbut quite difficult to detect attack, which may cause irreversible damage to the user due to the delay in discovery. Thus, the attack is capable of appearing at multiple layers, causing delay in data transfer. This delay may be extremely crucial in disaster management applications. The following sections in this chapter describe a technique for mitigating DOS attack in an IoT environment.

In this chapter, we show that there are several categories of intrusion detection schemes being used to mitigate DOS attacks in IoT environments. In Section 4.2, we discuss some of the well-known IDS before describing the basic idea behind the use of mobile agents (MA) in the IDS. The MAs allow us to take the load off from individual "things" and increase the lifetime of the "things."

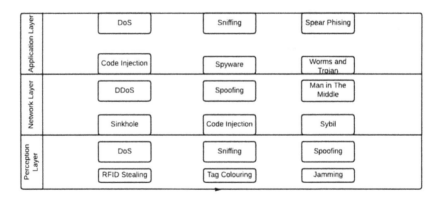

Figure 4.1 Attacks in IOT.

In Section 4.3, we define the layered reference framework of the IDS to be used in detecting DOS attacks in the IoT environment. In Section 4.4, we discuss the network model based on the De Bruijn graph. This section includes the reasons for choosing the De Bruijn graph for modeling the network.

Section 4.5 discusses the assumptions of the proposed IDS along with the definitions of basic terminologies. Section 4.6 includes a detail description of the proposed algorithm for black hole attack detection alongwith a case study

Section 4.7 describes the technique to detect the Denial of Service (DoS) attack.

Section 4.8 includes the result analysis. The final section is the concluding one.

4.2 Methods for Generic IDS and the Need for MAs

Behavior rule–based IDS approach has been discussed in the study by Sharma et al. [2]. This approach relies on the use of monitoring nodes to detect misbehaving nodes involved in zero-day attacks. However, they did not discuss about the parameters involved in measuring the performance efficiency of the system. There have also been recent IDS proposals on artificial system [3], clustering-based technology [4, 5], support vector machine (SVM) [6, 7], neural network [8–10], etc. Specifically, attacks such as jamming attacks, replay attack, etc., have been considered in the study by Fu et al. [12] to be mitigated using IoT networks based on an automata model.

Detection of malicious node using MA is a new direction for intrusion detection system. MAs are software agents [14] that have the capability to move from one host to another. Use of MA has several advantages, which help to overcome the limitation of most of the existing IDS in terms of increased lifetime and effectiveness of the underlying network. The MAs are created as smart software, which can act even in the absence of the host that initiated them. After completion of their assigned tasks, the MAs return to the host to report the result or simply terminate. The MAs are characterized by properties discussed in the study by Palmquis [16] as autonomy, rationality, social ability, inferential capability, etc. The autonomous nature of MA allows them to operate as independent entities. The rationality feature of MAs makes them able to analyze a problem to solve it. Due to the presence of inference capability, the MAs can share their knowledge in order to achieve a specific goal. The most important feature is social ability. This helps the agents to be able to meet and interact with other agents.

4.2.1 Why MAs?

There are several reasons why MAs are being used in IDS. A few of the main motivations are as follows:

- Delay caused by networks: The traditional hierarchical IDS often falls short of achieving on time detection of attacks due to communication delay. MAs, when they are used, respond faster, as they are directly dispatched from the central controller to the target host.
- Minimizing the network traffic: In traditional IDS, the central controller collects the data from different host machines and processes them to find any malicious behavior in the network. This may increase the network traffic, thus resulting a congestion overhead in the network. By employing MAs, the load on the network can be reduced as these MAs employ efficient search mechanisms thereby reducing the necessity for data traffic among several hosts.
- Persistency: As mobile nodes operate autonomously and asynchronously, they are not prone to failure even if the host, which initiated them, fails. This provides added advantage of employing MAs in IDS. In the case of the centralized machines, when the central controller fails, the entire IDS is considered to be down as there is no communication among other hosts.
- Structure and platform independence: Structure of MAs is not fixed. Depending on the requirement of the network, the structure may vary. The user can write their own program to find the attacker. Depending on the attack type, the functionality of MA may vary.
- Dynamic nature: The dynamic nature of MAs enables them to move around the network. This makes it possible to reconfigure the system during runtime also. MAs can be cloned,

dispatched or put to sleep when the network configuration has to be changed. Also, they can sense their execution environment and dynamically adapt to the situation.

- Heterogeneous environment: MAs can be interoperable on multiple platforms. This is possible because of the virtual interpreter installed on the host machine. MAs are generally computer- and transport layer–independent and are dependent only on the execution environment. This feature enables the MAs to be used on several different platforms without compatibility problems.
- Robust in nature: Even if one of the agents fails, the other agents in the IDS can take up the tasks of the failed agent and continue the detection. This robust behavior of MAs makes them more applicable in large environments where several agents and their interaction are needed for proper monitoring of the network.
- Scalability: With the help of distributed MA-based IDS, however, if the network grows larger, then it could be easily handled. Agents have the capability to clone and distribute themselves to the new machines when they are added to the network.

4.2.2 Main Issues in Implementing MA-Based IDS

Given all the characteristics of MAs as above, there remains certain challenges in implementing the intrusion detection system based on MAs. Following is a list of such challenges:

- Security: MAs require administration rights as they initiate response when an intrusion is identified. By granting an MA to access all information about the host it is operating on, an intruder can easily induce any virus. Some preliminary measures can be taken in order to alleviate these security problems. Some of them include providing limited access control to important resources, applying cryptographic methods to exchange information, etc.
- User privacy: One more potential problem involved is when the MA contains confidential information about the user. Some hosts might try to get the private information from the MAs, which contain client details.

- Delay: Observing the manner in which, the network attacks are increasing, it becomes obligatory on IDS to detect attacks immediately and report them spontaneously. If MAs are used to accomplish this, it results in reduced performance of the entire network.
- Efficiency: If the size of the coding of an MA is large enough, that may create some network overhead and reduce the efficiency of the network.

4.3 Reference Framework of MA-Based IDS

The layered architecture of MA-based IDS is shown in Figure 4.2. This reference framework is not explicitly implemented in all MA-based IDS for IoT systems; however, the fundamental blocks are conceptually relevant in order to understand the working of any such IDS. We thus analyze and understand all the parts of this framework.

Figure 4.2 shows the layer-wise functionality of MAs during their lifetime and also describes the jobs of agents at different layers. There are three categories of MAs performing specialized functions during their lifetime. At first, the host agent (HA) has to collect the raw data from the host machine. Then, functional agent (FA) computes the packet delivery ratio (P_{dr}). After computation, specialized agent compares the resultant P_{dr} with the predefined one and then gives responses to the source node accordingly.

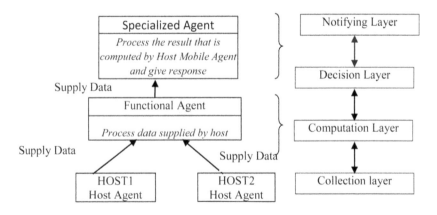

Figure 4.2 Framework of proposed Mobile Agent–based IDS.

4.4 Motivations for Using De Bruijn Graph for Network Modeling

We need to choose a topology for modeling the wireless sensor network, keeping in mind the characteristics required for implementing the IDS. It is understood that in order to enhance the efficiency of network, we must keep the number of outgoing edges from each host to a minimum level on careful investigation of different graph-based topologies, a few desirable traits of De Bruijn graphs make it a logical choice for investigation. In this model (Figure 4.3), the nodes with shortest path are connected through one hop.

The node sequence describes a set of nodes where the links among the nodes are created in such a way that when the node n with bit sequence $(a_0^n, a_1^n, a_2^n, \ldots a_k^n)$ is connected with a node m having a bit sequence $(a_0^m, a_1^m, a_2^m, \ldots a_k^m)$ where $1 \leq m$, $n \leq r-1$, then $(a_j^m = a_i^n + 1)$ where $0 \leq i, j \leq k-1$. Each node has in-degree and out-degree r. k is the diameter of the network. The rules for creating the network based on the De Bruijn graph are as follows:

1. There is a set of symbols SS and a number nn.
2. For each element of SnSn, we have a node, named as such – one for each sequence of symbols from SS of length nn. The same symbol can appear multiple times in the sequence.
3. When we can obtain the address of node vv from the address of node uu by removing the first symbol and appending a new symbol to the end, there is a path from uu to vv.

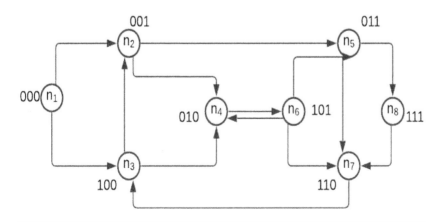

Figure 4.3   Network model following De Bruijn graph.

4.5 Definition

The following section includes the definitions of the terminologies used in the proposal of the IDS:

Packet Receive Counter: The number of packet that a node i receives from a neighbor node j is denoted as CPR $_{(i,j)}$(Packet Receive Counter), $1 \leq i, j \leq N$, where N is the total number of node in the network and $i \neq j$ and CPR $_{(i,j)} \geq 1$.

Packet Forward Counter: Total number of packet that a node i forwards to its neighbors j is defined as CPF $_{(i,j)}$ (Packet Forward Counter) where $1 \leq i, j \leq N-1$ and $i \neq j$.

Packet Delivery Ratio ($P_{dr(i,j)}$): This is defined as the ratio of CPF $_{(i,j)}$ (Packet Forward Counter) of each node i for each neighbor j to the CPR $_{(i,j)}$ (Packet Receive Counter), $1 \leq i, j \leq n$ and $i \neq j$.

$$CPR_{(i,j)} = CPR_{(i,j)} + 1 \qquad (4.1)$$

$$CPF_{(i,j)} = CPF_{(i,j)} + 1 \qquad (4.2)$$

$$P_{dr(i,j)} = CPF_{(i,j)}/CPR_{(i,j)} \qquad (4.3)$$

If this $P_{dr(i,j)} >$ THRESHOLDP$_{dr(i,j)}$, it marks the ith neighbor as malicious node and inform source node (Figure 4.4).

4.6 MA-Based IDS to Detect Black Hole Attack

The proposed IDS has the following assumptions:

1. A node interacts with its one-hop neighbors directly and with other nodes via intermediate nodes using multi-hop packet forwarding.

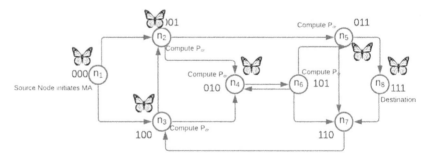

Figure 4.4   A network in normal condition – the MA moves from source node N_0 to destination node N_6 by the forward path.

2. Every node has a unique address as generated by the De Bruijn graph properties in the network.
3. The source node creates an MA with lifetime of maximum hop count to the destination.
4. Any node in the route from source to destination can create new MA if any malicious behavior is observed by it.

4.6.1 Algorithm and Flow Chart

This subsection includes algorithm for proposed black hole IDS using MA (Mobagent). This algorithm describes the tasks of MA (HA, FA) and that of specialized black agent. Both the agents are initiated by the source node. The FA is used to compute ratio of forwarding packets to receiving packets. Threshold calculation is also shown in this algorithm. The detection is done by the specialized black agent depending on the computation of the FA.

```
mobmove ()
   /* the mobmove() method is called whenever a new
network is created and a source send packet to the
destination */
Begin
The source node S is pushed into the stack
Until the stack is empty or goal node is reached
repeat
          pop a node from stack and mark as 'CN'
          look at the route table to find next node
          call the mobagent () to perform the operation
          push the node in the stack
mobagent ( )
   /* mobagent () method is called from mobmove() when
a new node is observed */
```

Count the numbers of packet forwarded by the node (P_f) and number of packets receive by the node (P_r)

```
          Calculate R=Pf/Pr
          Store node Id and R to mobstatus table
return to mobmove()
thresholdcalc ( )
   /*the source calculate the threshold value that is
compared when black agent moves to find malicious node
in the network*/
set i=1, Rtotal =0
```

```
until i<no. of intermediate hops from source to
destination(N)
    Read R_i from mobstatus table for i^th node
    R_total=R_total+R_i
    ThR = R_total/no. of intermediate hops (N) * T_delay
blackagent ()
    /*The source node invoke this agent when destination
node fails to acknowledge within Tout to the source
node */
    Observe R_i for i^th node
if R_i <ThR
    send MMSG (Malicious Message) to source node
else
    Decrease hops count by 1.
        If hop count=0
            Terminate execution
  end if
End
```

4.6.2 Case Study

Let us take the example of a network consisting of eight nodes (Figure 4.5). The forwarding path between source node S (colored YELLOW) and destination node D (colored BLUE) is marked by all GREEN nodes. All the other nodes in the network are denoted by WHITE color.

S creates an HA and forwards it through the forward path to the destination node D. The FA calculates the confidence ratio R which is the ratio of number of packet forwarded by the node i (P_f) to the next hop node in original route and number of packet received by the node i (P_r)

$$R^i = P_f^i/P_r^i, \dots\dots\dots\dots\dots\dots\dots\dots \quad (4.4)$$

where P_f^i is the total number of packets forwarded by the ith node and P_r^i is the number of packets received by the ith node.

In the absence of any malicious node, the destination node D receives the Mobagent (HA, FA) within timeout (T_{out}). The "NOINTRUD" signal is sent by D to the source node to confirm the absence of any intruder.

Figure 4.6 depicts the network under attack from a malicious node M. The source node S regenerates a Mobagent after waiting for a fixed

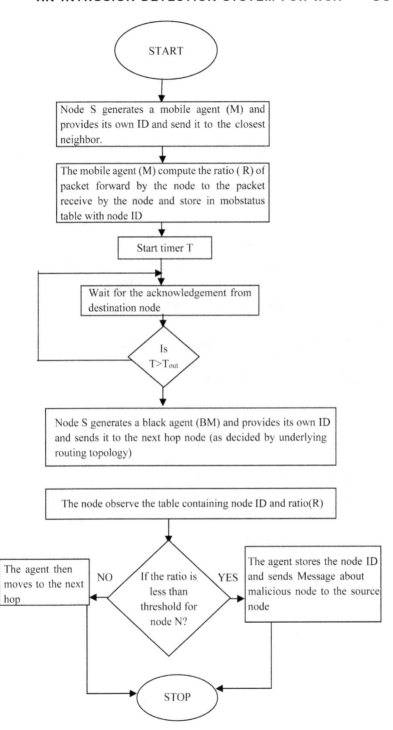

Figure 4.5   Flowchart showing the detection of black hole attack.

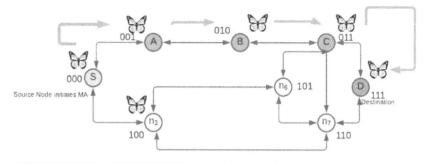

Figure 4.6   Source node creates Mobagent and sends it to the destination node.

interval of time (f) and sends it toward the destination node D. Now, the HA sends k data stream from malicious node to the next hop node E. As E is not a neighbor of D, so it does not have any route to D. E simply drops the packets that are coming for D. The HA waits till T_{out} for return data streams, increments the counter P_r and T_{delay} whenever a data stream is received back, and sets $P_f = k$. E does not process the packets that are coming from M, so it does not return any data stream to M. Here, value of P_f cannot be set by HA. Then, the FA calculates confidence ratio R^i for the ith node as follows:

$$R^i = \left(P_f^i / P_r^i\right) * \left(1/T_{delay}\right) \ldots \ldots \ldots \ldots \quad (4.5)$$

The black agent (specialized agent) observes that R^i is less than ThR^i, thus it readily informs the node A and the source node S (Figure 4.7).

Once the source node S receives message about malicious node (MMAL), it discards the previous path. It then sends RREQ (Route Request message) via a new path. Figures 4.8 and 4.9 describe this phenomenon. Finally, the new forward path S-I-F-G-D is established (Figure 4.10).

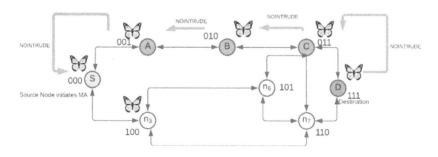

Figure 4.7   Destination node D sends acknowledgement to the source node S.

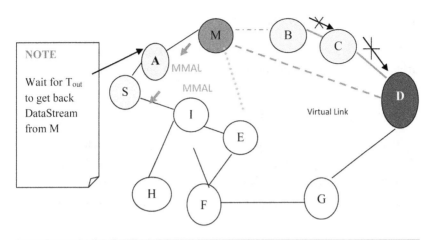

Figure 4.8   After a time period S sends another Mobagent for D.

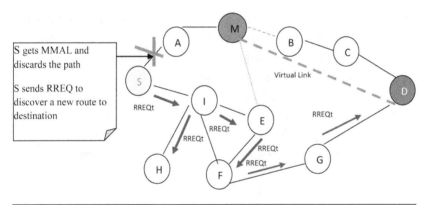

Figure 4.9   The source node S sends RREQ to create a new path with destination node D.

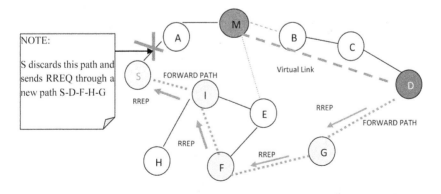

Figure 4.10   A new path is created with destination node D (S-I-F-G-D).

4.7 MA-Based IDS for DoS Attack

Let's now discuss the algorithm to prevent the network from DoS attack. The following assumptions are made in this regard:

4.7.1 Assumption

1. Every node has a unique ID in the network, which is assigned to a new node collaboratively by existing nodes.
2. The source node generates MA after a specific period of time.
3. The MA moves toward forward path created using RREQ and RREP.

4.7.2 DoS Attack

In Figure 4.11, it is observed that the source nodes N_0 generates the MA and sends it to the closest neighbor N_1. The MA at N_1 compute $CPR_{(i,j)}$ according to the Equation 4.1. MA then calculates $CPF_{(i,j)}$ using Equation 4.2 and then computes $P_{dr(i,j)}$ using Equation 4.3. If the $P_{dr(i,j)}$ is greater than $THRESHOLDP_{dr(i,j)}$, then MA readily informs the source node via the intermediate nodes. From Figure 4.11, it is observed that the MA reaches the destination node only when the network is free from DoS attack by a selfish node. The source uses the same path for others packets to be sent.

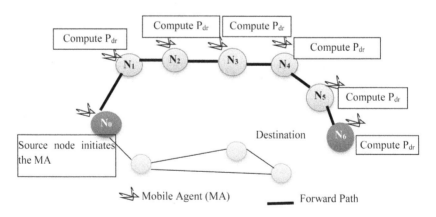

Figure 4.11   A network without malicious attack the MA moves from source node N_0 to destination node N_6 by the forward path.

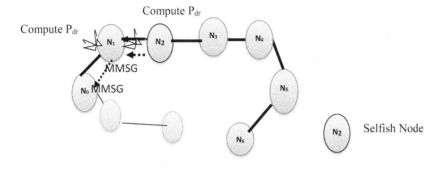

Figure 4.12   A network with the malicious attack.

The Figure 4.11 describes the situation when the network is under DoS attack by a selfish node. Here, the node N_2 acts as a malicious node. N_1 sends RREQ messages to the node N_2. The node N_2 is a node in the forward path from source to destination node. N_2 behaves as selfish node and refuse to forward packet to the neighbor node N_3. When the MA comes to the node N_2, it observes that the node behaves as malicious node by computing $P_{dr(N2, N3)}$. This value is greater than THRESOLDP$_{dr(N2, N3)}$, and it sends MMSG (malicious message) to the source node (Figure 4.12).

Following subsection describes the algorithm that depict the task of MA (HA, FA, specialized agent)

4.7.3 Algorithm and Flow Chart

This section consists of a proposed algorithm for detecting DoS attack in Mobile Adhoc Network. The algorithm describes the task of the MA for discovering the malicious node in MANET. The source node starts a timer during sending packets to the destination node. After receiving packets, the destination node sends an Acknowledgement (ACK) message to the source node. The source node waits till T_{out} for the acknowledgment signal ACK from destination node. In case the ACK is not received by the source node with the T_{out}, it initiates the mobile agents (HA, FA) and forwards them toward the destination node. The HA collects data from host machine and provides these data to FA who computes the ratio. Then, the specialized agent takes the decision about malicious node.

The flow chart pictorially represents the task of agents to detect DoS attack in MANET. The Mobagent is initiated by the source node.

```
/* The following algorithm depicts the task of a
mobile agent*/
Begin
        Send_packet(source,destination
        Start Timer T
        Until recv_ACK
        repeat
                T=T+1
        if T>Tout
                generate mobile agent
        Else
                Wait for ACK.
        End if
The mobile agent observe for ith node, the number of
packets received from
neighbor node j and compute CPR(i,j)
FA compute CPF(i,j)for the ith node
FA compute Pdr(i,j) for the ith node at tth instance
/*Job of specialized agent*/
If the ratio is more than threshold for ith node
                Then
                        The agent moves to the next hop node
                        Decrease hop count by 1
                Else
                        Agent reports the malicious activity
                        to the source node
        End if
End
```

4.7.4 Case Study

Let's take the scenario as described in section 7.3.

In the absence of any malicious node, the destination node D receives the Mobagent within T_{out}. The "NOINTRUD" signal is sent by D to the source node to confirm the absence of any intruder, as shown in Figure 4.15.

Figure 4.15 shows that the network is attacked by a malicious node M. The malicious node M receives all the packets from the source

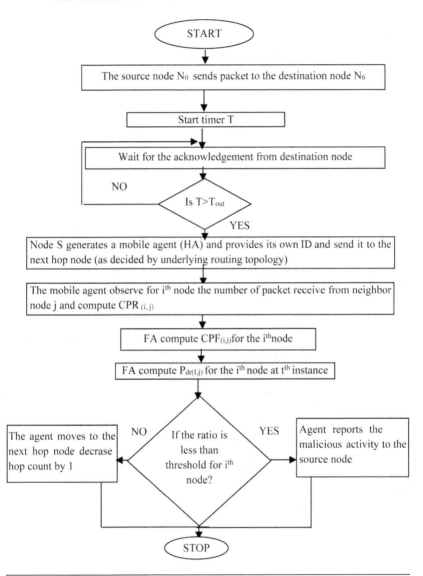

Figure 4.13 Flow diagram to show task of Mobile Agent.

node through intermediate hop A. The node M behaves maliciously and to prevent drainage of battery, it keeps silent. The packets that are coming from A for destination node D are not processed and forwarded by node M. Node M deny to provide service to the network. This is the scenario when the network is under DoS attack by a selfish node. When the source node delivers packets for destination node D,

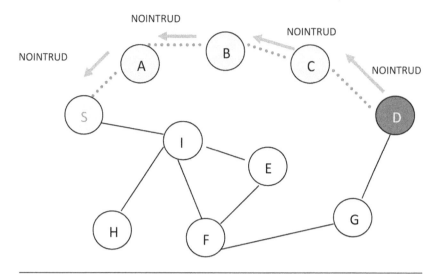

Figure 4.14 Destination node sends "NOINTRUD" signal to the source node.

it waits for ACK from D. After a period of time, the source node S generates a Mobagent (HA, FA) and sends it for destination node D.

The agents that are initiated by the source node collects the data from host A and compute P_{dr} for A, then moves to the next hop node M and again compute P_{dr} for M. As the node M is selfish, so it does not forward the agents to the next node. Now, the source node S creates a specialized agent and forward through the path.

The specialized agent observes the P_{dr} value for each node and compares it with the THRESOLDP$_{dr}$. When it finds that for node M this ratio is less, the agents readily inform source node S through

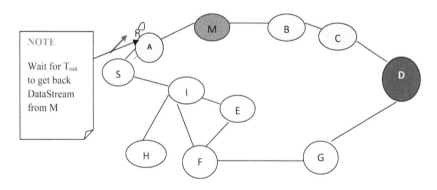

Figure 4.15 After a time period S sends another Mobagent for D.

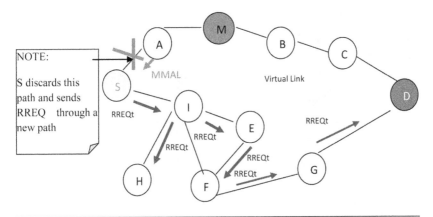

Figure 4.16 Source node creates a new path to the destination node D.

MMAL message about malicious node. The source node S discards the path and sends new RREQ for new route through S-I-F-G, as shown in Figure 4.16.

4.8 Performance Analysis

In this section, the performance evaluation of proposed algorithm is given. The performance evaluation is done based on some metric that are also described here. Simulation parameters are also listed in this section. In performance evaluation, comparative plots are shown to depict that this proposed algorithm works better than existing IDS.

4.8.1 Performance Metric

Packet throughput (P_{Th}): This is defined as the ratio between the numbers of packets generated by the application layer sources (P_s) and the number of packets received by the sink at the final destination (P_d),

$$\text{i.e., } P_{Th} = P_d/P_s \tag{4.6}$$

Node mobility (N_m): It is defined as the transition rate of a node within a network and is given by,

$$N_m = Dist_{node}/Time \tag{4.7}$$

Cumulative sum of receiving packet: This is defined as the sequence of partial sums of all packets received by the destination node.

$$CU_{Sum} = \sum_{i=1}^{n} N_{pkt}^{i} \qquad (4.8)$$

where n is the total number of packets, which sends at i^{th} instance to the destination node.

End-to-end delay (D): The-end-to-end delay (D) is defined as the time of reception of the packet by the destination node (T_d) and the time of generation of the packet by the source node (T_s) for a sequence of packet P_{seq}.

For the packet sequence P^1_{seq} $D_1 = T^1_d - T^1_s$
For the packet sequence P^2_{seq} $D_2 = T^2_d - T^2_s$
For the packet sequence P^n_{seq} $D_n = T^n_d - T^n_s$

$$D = \frac{\sum_{i=1}^{n} Di}{Npkt} \qquad (4.9)$$

where $D_i = D_1 + D_2 + D_3 \ldots + D_n$ and N_{pkt} is the total number of packets.

P_{dr}: This is the ratio between the number of packets received by the sink at the final destination (P_d) and the numbers of packets originating from the application layer sources (P_s).

$$P_r = \frac{P_d}{P_s} \qquad (4.10)$$

4.8.2 Performance Evaluation of DoS Attack Detection (MADSN)

Figure 4.17 describes the throughput of packet delivery over time. As is observed, the presence of any malicious node in the network results in performance degradation of the network. When the network is under attack in the presence of MA-based IDS, the performance of the network remains at par as in the case of the network without attack. This implies that MA-based IDS can readily detect the malicious node and help to maintain the performance consistently.

Figure 4.18 shows the effect of packet size on end-to-end delay. The series "a" and "b" indicates the performance in the presence of attacker and in the presence of both attacker and IDS, respectively.

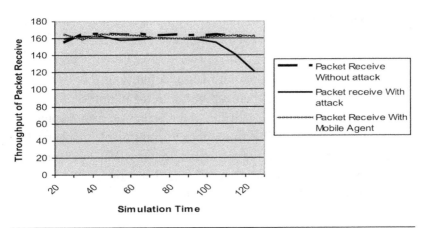

Figure 4.17 Throughput of packet receive when the network is under attack and in presence of Mobile Agent.

Both the series show that the end-to-end delay increases as the packet size increases. The performance is better when an IDS is present in network. The peak of the graph denotes that at that instance of time, the source and destination nodes come closer to each other and thus the distance of source–destination and source–adversary nodes may become same. In such scenario, the MA-based IDS does not perform well and thus cause high end-to-end delay. Network congestion overhead and IDS computational complexity overrules the efficiency of MA-based IDS.

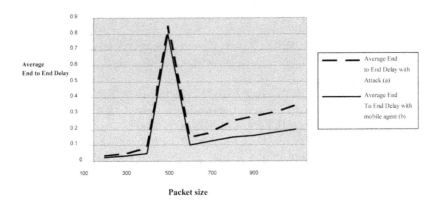

Figure 4.18 End-to-end delay vs. packet size.

4.9 Conclusion

The frameworks for intrusion detection proposed in this chapter takes care of two of the most dangerous attacks in the wireless sensor network layer of an IoT system. These two attacks have the potential to disrupt network traffic along with confidentiality of the data generated at the source due to their capacity to remain 'unseen' for a long time. We have used the De Bruijn graph structure for mapping the dynamic nature of the WSN to an efficient and scalable topology. This has proved to be useful in the consistent performance of our proposed IDS frameworks. The mobile agent-based detection has helped us to increase network lifetime as well as detection time.

References

1. Chaabouni, N.; Mosbah, M.; Zemmari, A. Cyrille sauvignac and parvez faruki "network intrusion detection for IoT security based on learning techniques". IEEE Communications Surveys and Tutorials November 2018, 00, 0.
2. Sharma, V.; You, I.; Chen, R.; Cho, J.H. BRIoT: Behavior rule specification-based misbehavior detection for IoT-embedded cyber-physical systems. IEEE Access 2019, 7, 118556–118580.
3. Yang, Z.; Ding, Y.; Jin, Y.; Hao, K. Immune-endocrine system inspired hierarchical coevolutionary multiobjective optimization algorithm for IoT service. IEEE Trans. Cybern. 2020, 50, 164–177.
4. Umar, R.; Zhang, X.; Wang, W.; Khan, R.U.; Kumar, J.; Sharif, A. A multimodal malware detection technique for Android IoT devices using various features. IEEE Access 2019, 7, 64411–64430.
5. Zhang, Y.; Wang, K.; Gao, M.; Ouyang, Z.; Chen, S. LKM: A LDA-based k-means clustering algorithm for data analysis of intrusion detection in mobile sensor networks. Int. J. Distrib. Sens. Netw. 2015, 13.
6. Wang, H.; Gu, J.; Wang, S. An effective intrusion detection framework based on SVM with feature augmentation. Knowl.-Based Syst. 2017, 136, 130–139.
7. Shen, M.; Tang, X.; Zhu, L.; Du, X.; Guizani, M. Privacy-preserving support vector machine training over blockchain-based encrypted IoT data in smart cities. IEEE IoT J. 2019, 6, 7702–77.
8. Subba, B.; Biswas, S.; Karmakar, S. A neural network based system for intrusion detection and attack classification. In Proceedings of the 2016 Twenty Second National Conference on Communication (NCC), Guwahati, India, 4–6 March 2016; pp. 1–6.
9. Barreto, R.; Lobo, J.; Menezes, P. Edge Computing: A neural network implementation on an IoT device. In Proceedings of the 2019

5th Experiment International Conference, Funchal (Madeira Island), Funchal, Portugal, 12–14 June 2019; pp. 244–246.

10. Leem, S.G.; Yoo, I.C.; Yook, D. Multitask learning of deep neural network-based keyword spotting for IoT devices. IEEE Trans. Consum. Electr. 2019, 65, 188–194.

11. Razaa, S.; Wallgrena, L.; Voigta, T. baSwedish, "SVELTE: Real-time Intrusion Detection in the Internet of Things" available at http://www. cs.umanitoba.ca/~comp7570/assets/media/0404Singh_M.pdf accessed on 15th/05/2017.

12. Fu, Y.; Yan, Z.; Cao, J.; Koné, O.; Xuefei. "An Automata Based Intrusion Detection Method for Internet of Things." 2017, available at https://www.hindawi.com/journals/misy/2017/1750637/ accessed on 13th/05/2017.

13. Elike, H.; Xavier, B.; Andrew, H.; PierreLouis, D.; Ephraim, I.; Christos, T.; Robert, A. "Threat analysis of IoT networks Using Artificial Neural Network Intrusion Detection System", available at https://arxiv.org/ftp/ arxiv/papers/1704/1704.02286.pdf accessed on 15th/05/2017.

14. Wayne, J.; Peter, M.; Tom, K.; Don, M. "Applying Mobile Agents to Intrusion Detection and Response", NIST Interim Report (IR) – 6416 October 1999.

15. Hu, Y.-C.; Perrig, A.; Johnson, D. B. Wormhole attacks in wireless networks. IEEE J. Sel. Areas Commun. IEEE J SEL AREA COMM 2006, 24, 2, 370–380.

16. Palmquis, Y. Intelligent agents in computer and network management. Course paper, Texas University, 1998. http://www.gslis.utexas. edu/~palmquis/courses/project98/agents/webpage.html.

17. Chaki, R.; Bhattacharya, U. A new scalable optimal topology for multihop optical network. Comput. Commun., Elsevier 2005, 28, 5, 557–570.

5

AN NLP-BASED SCHEME FOR USER DATA SECURITY FROM OVERPRIVILEGED IoT APPS

RITUPARNA CHAKI

University of Calcutta, Kolkata, West Bengal, India

Contents

5.1 Introduction

Breaking news on possible breach of cybersecurity in a power grid hits the news media in early March of 2021 [1]. Is this just another page-3 story from the news media? Well, some raw facts and a possible technical analysis do not allow us to safely assume that.

A new study says that some overseas attackers may have targeted power facilities across India last year in the middle of hostilities at the border. A massive power outage in Mumbai in October 2020, stopping suburban trains and shutting down hospitals and the stock exchange for hours, could be due to some undesired activities by a group of hackers, says the report that has been shared with the government.

In a statement, the Power Ministry confirmed their knowledge on the state operation, a major foreign country to use malware to penetrate India's smart power grid. The intruders may have planted the malware in the key power plants in India, as reported by the New York Times. The flow of the malware was detected by Recorded Future, a US-based company. They have analyzed the online digital threats to find that most of the malware was never activated! A total of 21 IP addresses linked to 12 Indian organizations in the power generation and transmission sector – classified as critical – were targeted.

The incident sited above indicates that, as we move toward maximum connectedness with a global coverage, we are faced with multiple security threats. We have already studied the types of common errors and intrusions in the Internet of Things (IoT), leading to catastrophic failures. It is obvious that IoT security is a multilayer phenomenon, where specialized algorithms need to be deployed at different layers to manage the vulnerabilities to which the respective layers are susceptible. Figure 5.1 shows a modular diagram of the layer-wise perception of the IoT environment.

We have already discussed about the several attack types targeting the base layer comprising of wireless sensor networks. Let's take a look at the vulnerabilities of an IoT-based system at different layers, as shown in Figure 5.2.

Providing support for security only on lower layers of IoT is not enough to provide complete security support for end users. Most IoT systems rely on an application layer, such as an enabler app, for providing the expected service to the end user. The main function of the application layer in the IoT networks include securing user data by restricting the app from accessing different services. These apps have built-in mechanisms to behave in a "user-friendly" manner. These apps ask for special permissions prior to installing them. The main idea behind seeking these permissions is to make the

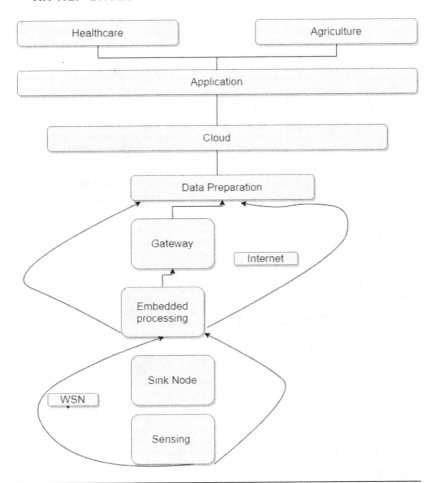

Figure 5.1   The layer-wise composition of IoT.

Figure 5.2   A depiction of layer-wise vulnerabilities of an IoT environment.

user aware of the access privileges of the app. The user, however, never bothers (in general) to carefully check the approvals being sought and hit the "OK" button in a hurry to get their desired tasks done.

In this chapter, the focus is on the end-point security. By end-point security, we consider to protect the user from security attacks by malicious applications that act as enablers of IoT services. The breach to user data security is attained through the seemingly innocent permissions sought during installation of these apps. We address the concern that the grant of permissions without appropriate awareness of the concerned user have the possibility to turn into serious privacy breaches.

In Section 1 (this section), we describe the organization of the paper. In Section 2, we give a detailed description of the project/the problem we are trying to solve. This can include a brief history as well as the specifications for the project. In Section 3, we describe what we accomplished. In Section 4, we critique our results, including a comparison with other systems/work in the area. In Section 5, we discuss our future work.

5.1.1 Challenges of End-Point Security

Since the expansion of IoT has reached every aspect of humanity, it is obvious that the end-point applications are being deployed as mobile apps mostly based on Android or iOS. The areas of applications are as diverse as possible; some examples are smart home, smart power grids, smart traffic management, smart healthcare, smart farming, etc.

We consider here the specific security vulnerabilities of IoT involving context-based, cross-device and automatic operations. From the user's viewpoint, there are a few sources of expectations about an app's performance. Prior to installing an app, a user checks the user manual document associated with an app. This manual is written using natural language descriptions and the certificate contains the details about the app's behavior. Installation of an app generally involves permitting a set of tasks as requested by the app. It has been seen that these permissions are useful in protecting user

We collect information about your activity in our services, which may include:

- Views and interactions with content and ads.
- People with whom you communicate or share content.
- Which data sets you view or download.

Figure 5.3 Part of an App's privacy policy asking for unusual permission.

data as they restrict certain operations while permitting a specific set of operations to be performed. However, the analysis of permission at runtime is a challenging task. The documents related to permission on Android/IOS platform are normally too big in size and contain limited information about the permission itself. In order to write generic permission documents, the developers often include extra permissions, leading to overprivileged applications. Figure 5.3 shows a part of privacy policy for an educational app.

The second point about the information being collected by the app might be done with questionable intentions. Why would an app be interested to know about the user's educational personal communications? There is the possibility that this might be done with an intention to track unauthorized use of data by the users. There is also the possibility that this is just one of the "additional privileges" of the app. Often, these overprivileged features of an app lead to user data breaches by malware. The available documentation strategies for permission seeking are not enough for mobile device users to make informed decision-making about a particular app's security breaches.

A very simple example of smart assistant interface is shown in Figure 5.4. This shows a subset of tasks being performed by a health-care app. All the tasks in Figure 5.3 requires sensors for data collection, and this is done using either Android/IoS support. The users are often naive enough to believe that the information being collected by such apps are being used only for his/her benefits. In reality, however, the users might be sharing too much personal information with unknown entities.

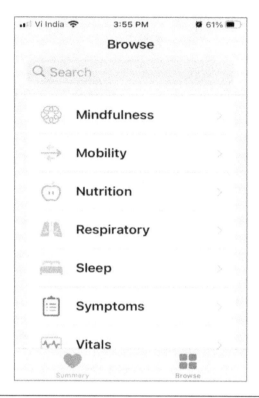

Figure 5.4 Example of healthcare application.

For example, a user of a smart watch or a smart headphone is not even aware of the variety of information about him being collected by the devices. It is important to understand that as a user of a smart device, the privacy of user data remains extremely vulnerable to unintended access. Most of the voice-enabled IOT services have the potential to turn malicious by their promiscuous (always ON and listen) mode of operation. The users of the voice assistant are generally not fully aware of the privacy risks and are not even using existing privacy controls effectively.

5.2 Machine Intelligence and NLP to Secure User Data

Of late, machine intelligence techniques are gaining popularity for embedding intelligence in the IoT networks in order to deal with the variety of security threats. The obvious choice of technique is through natural language processing, or NLP. Researchers have been fascinated by the domain of speech recognition and audio-response generation related to the IoT system.

NLP involves text processing and semantic analysis; these are achieved through word similarity measure. The correctness of spoken words is best judged in the context of usage. This is where the word similarity measures are useful as they measure the degree of closeness of words.

Researchers have been actively involved in studying the context of spoken commands to devices within an IoT environment. In the voice-controlled smart devices of present age, NLP is used to understand important linguistic concepts such as syntax and semantics. The context is important in distinguishing security-sensitive command from security-insensitive command. Thus, in a voice command–based verification by a bank, a spoken password by the user is compared with prestored patterns from the user. The prestored patterns are generated by a user while talking to the smart bot without even uttering a keyword!

Let's take the example of Olli, [1] a self-driving vehicle brought to market by Local Motors, which is one of IoT's popular applications with a device interface that uses NLP. In the instance of Olli, the use of natural language recognition helps to create a relationship between the passenger and the vehicle. The challenge in implementing such systems lies in the importance to understand the user's speech correctly, to be consistent with the word, and to identify the authentic user.

Besides speech recognition, the key components which play crucial roles in the use of NLP in user commands to activate systems like Alexa or Google home, etc., is the most common form of user input in IoT. It is obvious that such systems need to learn continuously from the user's (registered) commands to keep it updated with the changing perspectives of users. It is observed that such systems are vulnerable to attacks, such as replay, as they use an earlier recorded part of user's speech to mask the attacker from the authentication service.

There have been two main categories of studies into the application of NLP for securing IoT systems:

i. NLP in securing user data from unintended use by mobile device–based apps
ii. NLP in user authentication in voice-controlled IoT systems

In this chapter, the focus is to find the points of difference between the app's description and actual capabilities. The features of NLP are useful in this regard as they are helpful in extracting the meaning of security policy from an app description (free text). Once the exact meaning is extracted, it is compared with the actual capability of the app, obtained from its source code, by using NLP techniques.

As shown in the Figure 5.5, we have numerous IoT-based applications designed to allow healthcare professionals to collect information about a user's exercise patterns, activity, water intake, suggest dietary requirements, etc. The user goes through the features as offered by the app and decides to install it as the app does not clearly say anything about user privacy. The user in general does not have an easy access to the source code of the app to check about the inherent security vulnerabilities of the app. Very few users take the pain of going through user reviews before installing an app – thus exposing themselves to malicious apps.

In the following sections, we consider permission documents and large app descriptions for feature extraction with NLP techniques. We also consider crowdsourced user reviews, which provide an actual reflection of the performance by the app being

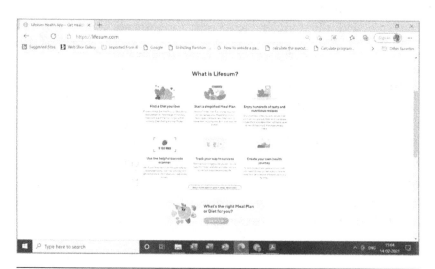

Figure 5.5 The opening screen of an app.

considered, for thematic features. Statistical topic modeling is employed for obtaining the actual sense out of the permissions sought by an app.

5.3 NLP Basics Revisited

What specific functions does your project accomplish for its users? Before going into the detail description of the framework for security analysis, let's have a look into the basics of NLP techniques that will be useful to understand the framework of the proposed CFCRGen system.

5.3.1 *Tokenization*

This is the process of segmenting a text document into "tokens," which are nothing but words, numbers, punctuation marks, etc. This is done before any processing of the text document to mark the meaningful basic units. These basic units are necessary to perform any analysis of the text. The resulting tokens are then used for the process of lemmatization.

5.3.2 *Stop Word Removal*

Stop words are the common words which are not of much importance toward the overall meaning of a sentence. Examples of such words are "the," "he," "have," etc. In order to reduce the size of the data set, we need to remove the stop words. This would lead to reduced training time as the number of tokens reduces. The stop-word list is prepared based on the number of times each word has appeared in a specific text. This is called the collection frequency. Then, the most frequently occurring terms (chosen on the basis of their semantic content) are added to the stop word list. These stop words are then removed during indexing.

5.3.3 *Lemmatization*

In NLP, lemmatization is the process of converting a word to its meaningful base word by considering the context. Lemmatization considers the full vocabulary of a language to perform a morphological analysis on words. The inflectional endings are removed, and the vase word, called lemma, is obtained. In case same words with different meanings are encountered, the parts of speech (POS) tagging is employed to extract the appropriate meaning.

5.3.4 LSA Topic Model

Traditionally, topic modeling in software engineering has been used to analyze source code, change logs, bug databases and execution traces. Topic modeling is an unsupervised task whereby topics are induced from actual data. Let's take the example of a privacy document with "car" and "race." We may infer that the document belongs to the topic of cars. Similarly, another document having commonly occurring words such as "patient," "medicine" belongs to the topic of patients. User reviews may be topically grouped as "financial," "casual," "professional," etc.

The process of topic modeling involves a statistical analysis of words in each text document among a set of documents. As an output of topic modeling, we obtain (a) topic-wise clusters of co-occurring words, (b) frequency distribution of document-wise topics and (c) a histogram of words per topic.

One of the common topic modeling techniques is Latent Semantic Analysis (LSA), also called LSI. This model assumes Gaussian distribution of terms. The output of LSA constitutes a semantic space of related words and documents, placed near one another.

5.3.5 SVM-BDT

This technique is used as a classifier in multi-class problems. The common support vector machine classifier enhanced with binary decision tree (SVM-BDT) [2] is tree-based architecture which contains binary SVM in the non-leaf nodes. The uniqueness of this architecture is that it takes advantage of both the efficient computation of the tree architecture and the high classification accuracy of SVMs. It has been seen that the use of this architecture results in training N-1 SVMs for an N-class problem, whereas only log2N SVMs (average case) are required to be consulted to classify a sample. Thus, SVM-BDT combination has better speed of recognition in case of problems with big number of classes.

5.4 Description of Proposed Algorithm for Analyzing App Behavior

The proposed logic is based on NLP techniques along with machine learning for detection of malicious activity by IoT Apps. NLP is used for thematic feature extraction. Machine learning involves classification and training of the system to generate response.

The security policy of an app is deduced from its free-text description. It is important to identify the various POS used in the description and find the relation between them. In order to understand the corelation between different POS, the dependencies are identified from the written description. For example, in the phrase "follow the patient," the noun "patient" is an accusative object of "follow" verb.

The CFCRGen algorithm consists of three phases as follows:

- Phase one involves tokenization followed by the use of NLP preprocessing techniques on the user review documents as well as the app description (.apk) and privacy documents. The output of this stage will generate a stream of phrases devoid of stop words and spaces.
- In phase two, we apply Lemmatization followed by topic modeling for generating semantic tags from the feature documents.
- Phase three will classify the apps into groups of suspect and trusted apps based on comparison between the user reviews and app descriptions.

5.4.1 Phase 1: Preprocessing

We have observed that with the increase in the popularity of IoT, it has become extremely easy for malicious App developers to collect information about user's calendars, contacts, browser histories, profile information, social streams, short messages or exact geographic locations. Some of the common install-time permissions which are granted without much thought are "have full network access," "view network connection," "prevent phone from sleeping," etc. It is obvious that these permissions may lead to user security vulnerability in more than one way.

In order to check the features of the app minutely, we use standard techniques in information retrieval (IR) and NLP to preprocess the application description. Initially, for the purpose of analyzing, we apply tokenization of the text into individual words and phrases up to four words in length. The text is split into sentences, and the sentences are then split into words. These words are then converted to lowercase and all punctuation marks are removed.

Once tokenization is completed, we begin the task of text preprocessing. This step would involve preparing text data to enable the computer to perform later tasks such as analysis, predictions, etc. After tokenization, we concentrate on the stop word removal. Stop words are words such as "be," "back," "backed," etc., which appear too frequently in a text. We have excluded stop words in order to focus on the words which are helpful in defining the actual meaning of the text. Then, we are left with a smaller set of meaningful tokens. The initial analysis of the description text is done by using the JMP text mining software which generates a number of the most frequently occurring words and phrases. Then, the frequently occurring words like "the," "and," etc., are deleted while processing the text from the word list. The JMP software uses a standard list of these stop words. The most frequently occurring words in the text are added to the stop word list for more clarity in the topics. Figure 5.6 shows some of the most frequently occurring words and phrases after stop words were removed from a few of the apps considered. Normally, there are several frequently occurring phrases in the document that illustrate the nature of app. For example, one of

App	Frequently occur-ring words	Count
Car Rac-ing	car, speed, race, fast, super, control, ...	1100, 123, 510, ...
Music	file, download, au-dio, music, genre,	2000, 1300, ...
E-shopping	shop, brand, color, buy, category, ...	200, 3000, 4000, 200, 82
Web	keyword, history, url, ad, ...	.....
Health	Diet, sleep, exer-cise, water, pulse , ...	.....
....	....	

Figure 5.6 Common attributes after removal of stop words.

the most frequently occurring phrases in a car racing manual is "struck a road divider." This indicates that common accidents at racing track occur between a car and a road divider.

5.4.2 Phase 2: Topic Modeling for Theme Extraction

The output text stream from the previous phase is now subjected to topic modeling for feature vector generation. Topic modeling is a machine learning algorithm used to extract the main topics from a large collection of text files. This technique is helpful in discovering hidden topics from a large collection of text documents. These extracted topics are then used to classify the set of .apk files. However, this model suffers from the overhead of complexity of analysis. Another problem is that it does not consider the linguistics aspect of text and thus fails to accurately analyze the text. Thus, we use it in combination with lemmatization – one of the key steps of NLP. Lemmatization is used to remove semantic duplicates. The output of lemmatization consists of more topic-related words for improved understanding.

After lemmatization, we use LSA for topic modeling. LSA uses the similar terms of text and related terms for thematic insights about a collection of documents. It uses the document-term matrix, which is an m × n matrix of m documents and n words (vocabulary) having term frequency (TF)–inverse document frequency (IDF) score, for this purpose. TF-IDF is a statistical measure for calculating the relevance of a word in a document among a collection of documents. The TF counts the number of times a word appears in a document. The IDF of a word lets us know how common or rare is the word in the collection of documents. Words such as "if," "what," "as," etc., are commonly occurring ones without much significance, hence their rank would be low. The IDF is obtained by dividing total document count by the number of documents containing a specific word and doing the log. Thus, the IDF closer to 0 means it is a common word, whereas IDF closer to 1 depicts its rarity. The TF-IDF score of a word is then obtained by multiplying these two numbers. The output of LSA is a set of probability values for a document to be having a specific theme. As in the paper [3], it is assumed that an app belongs to a specific theme if the respective probability is greater than or equal to 5%.

Next, the feature vector is generated by combining the themes from app description and the themes from app reviews. Thus, each element in the feature vector set is of the form <app_desc_theme, app_Capability>. This will lead the user to the observation that the apps with common theme-capability grouping are safe and those with uncommon theme-capability grouping are most likely malicious. The process is depicted in Figure 5.7.

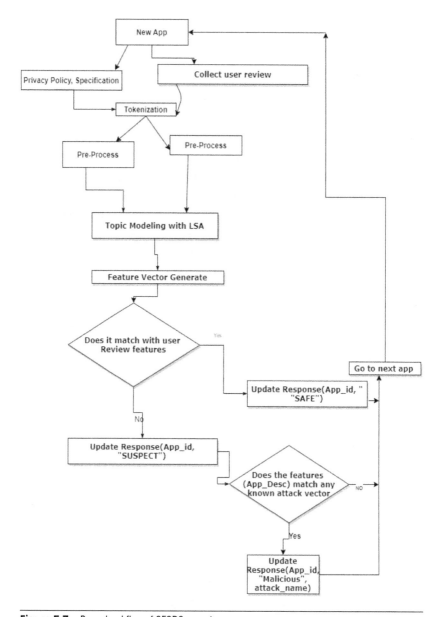

Figure 5.7   Procedural flow of CFCRGen system.

5.4.3 *Phase 3: Classifier Learner*

We use unsupervised learning to flag outliers in the feature set. These outliers, if not detected in time, can lead to anomalous behavior by the app, thus causing security breach. We use SVM-BDT for classification. SVM is chosen as it considers the relationships between the features contrary to other algorithms such as Naive Bayes. The BDT is well-known for its efficiency. Thus, the combination of BDT with the highly accurate SVM leads to a faster and accurate classification. It has been shown that utilizing this combination, N-1 SVMs had to be trained for an N-class problem, but the at-most $|log2N|$ SVMs are to be consulted for accurately classifying a sample [SVM-BDT-Based Intelligent Fingerprint Authentication System using Geometry Approach]. The classifier will take the feature vector set generated earlier as the input. In this manner, the learner learns to distinguish between the app_desc_theme and app_capability theme corresponding to malicious from those corresponding to safe applications. The SVM-BDT technique will recursively divide the feature vectors into two disjoint groups in each node of the decision tree. The SVM is then trained to decide the group membership for an unknown sample. We choose Cosine similarity to measure the distance between the classes. Cosine similarity has an advantage over the more popular Euclidean distance measure in cases where the similarities are far apart (due to size) but have a small angle among them. The similarity increases as the angle becomes smaller. The class with the smallest angle with one of the clustering groups is obtained and assigned to the respective class. The process continues till there is only a single class per group that defines the leaf node of the decision tree. As an example, let us consider the case of a messaging application S1 which uses permissions such as "uses the local network to allow you to directly transfer your account to a new phone." Besides messaging, this actually calls for sensitive API methods for accessing the local network of the user. This is an uncommon behavior captured by the SVM-BDT technique to warn the user about the probable malicious attack.

5.5 Conclusions

The idea of using NLP in end-point security in IoT environments has been discussed in this chapter. The IoT environment is a heterogeneous network comprising of fairly different types of networks and devices. Each layer of IoT has specific security vulnerabilities. Here, we have considered the end-point security, whereby the apps through which a user has rendered the IoT services are checked for maliciousness. The common techniques of verifying the app's permission set, against its actual capacity, do not consider the user ratings. In this chapter, the readers are presented with the novel idea of thematic classification of apps from their permission set, followed by grouping with their actual capabilities, finally checking against the user reviews to certify the app as malicious or safe. This is a fairly new domain which involves the use of different NLP techniques to process the fairly large text documents pertaining to user permissions. The proposed approach may be evaluated using real data set from Google Play.

References

1. "Mumbai Outage Example of China Targeting India Power Facilities: Report", NDTV; Reported by Vishnu Som; Ed. by Deepshikha Ghosh. Updated: March 01, 2021 5:47 pm IST.
2. "Ensembles of Binary SVM Decision Trees", Gjorgji Madjarov, Dejan Gjorgjevikj and TomcheDelev, ICT Innovations 2010 Web Proceedings ISSN 1857-7288, pp. 181–188.
3. "Active Semi-supervised Approach for Checking App Behavior against Its Description," S. Ma, S. Wang, D. Lo, R. H. Deng and C. Sun, 2015 IEEE 39th Annual Computer Software and Applications Conference, Taichung, Taiwan, 2015, pp. 179–184, doi:10.1109/ COMPSAC.2015.93.

Index

V

Value Sensitive Design 63
Virus 18

W

Water distribution systems 5
Weakness 8

Wearable sensors 4
Worms 20

CPSIA information can be obtained
at www.ICGtesting.com
Printed in the USA
JSHW022029090522
25519JS00001B/45